Sitcom

A Teacher's Guide

Julie Patrick

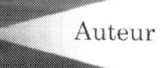

Julie Patrick

is a teacher of Media and Film at Ryburn Valley High School in West Yorkshire. She also delivers external courses to teachers and students and has co-written the specification for the new Film Studies GCSE from WJEC.

Acknowledgements

With thanks to Jackie Newman. Without you I would never have started this book. Thanks for being my mentor and my friend.

And Dan - without you I would never have finished this book! Thank you for your patience, understanding and just for being you.

This book is dedicated to my Dad, Clarry Patrick, the best Dad a girl could wish for.

All stills are courtesy of UKTV / BBC / image.net, except those on pages 20 (*Hancock's Half Hour*), 67 (*Friends*) and 79 (*Butterflies*), courtesy BFI Stills.

First Published 2007
by Auteur

The Old Surgery, 9 Pulford Road, Leighton Buzzard, Bedfordshire LU7 1AB. Tel: 01525 373896

© Auteur Publishing, 2007

All rights reserved. No part of this publication may be reproduced in any material form (including photocopying or storing it in any medium by electronic means and whether or not transiently or incidentally to some other use of this publication) without the written permission of the copyright owner.

ISBN: 978-1-903663-75-2

Auteur on the internet: http://www.auteur.co.uk

Designed and typeset by Active Media Publishing. www.ampublishing.net

Printed by The Direct Printing Company, Saxon Fields, Old Harborough Road, Brixworth, Northants, NN6 9BX

Contents

1. An Introduction to Sitcom

I'm Alan Partridge

Discussions regarding humour and the moving image will always feature disagreements about what is and isn't funny. What leaves one person rolling around helpless on the floor will have another staring blankly at a screen incongruously. However, there are specific comic strategies that all comedy uses to make audiences laugh and situation comedies will use a combination of different techniques and strategies to attract different target audiences.

In this *Guide* I want to explore connections between different comedy forms and, at the same time, offer you something tangible that you can enjoy reading and use in the classroom. I will therefore be examining closely the social and historical context of various situation comedies; early programmes and developments in the genre; and the stars and writers that are well established names in television comedy.

I will also consider different devices that situation comedy actors use to amuse audiences. I will focus on representation and make some comparisons between British and American situation comedies. I will look at the various structures of situation comedies, and what typical codes and conventions are used.

Throughout this *Guide* I will make detailed references to a wide range of different situation comedies that are in some way significant to developments in the form. My main aim is to offer topics and suggestions to open up discussions in the classroom, so I have included a wide range of programmes and open ended themes to enable this. This *Guide* won't provide all the answers but hopefully it will get your students asking the right questions.

Genre

Genre refers to three ways of understanding a media text – the audience reception, the structure of the text and the production process. Therefore, audiences look for codes and conventions in situation comedy that are recognisable as that genre; and they maintain this understanding through comparing the form to other genres. Producers respond to audiences' expectations and create appropriate comedy programmes that they can recognise easily as situation comedies as opposed to other comedy forms, such as sketch shows or comedy drama.

Unusually with genre, the sitcom contains quite a rigid structure, though I would argue 'comedy drama' and 'situation comedy' sometimes cross over. The length of series and programmes, performance style, themes, structure and the use of the camera, sound and *mise-en-scène* are all often clearly recognisable as a sitcom; which is probably why Taflinger could define three types of sitcom so clearly (see pg. 8).

However, this does not mean that the sitcom genre is easy to define and analyse as, typically of genre, new programmes come along that challenge our expectations of what a sitcom is through their use of narrative, structure or comic strategies. Programmes like *The Office*, for example, have challenged our expectations of style by using a documentary filming and performance style; *The Mighty Boosh* mixes strange characters and plots, with music and narration. As with all genres, the sitcom has had to evolve to suit modern audiences, which is one of the reasons for the debate around whether this genre can still thrive – has it changed so significantly that it is unrecognisable?

Hybrids

The League of Gentlemen

The situation comedy has also developed hybrid versions of itself, blending with genres like horror and science-fiction to create some humorous parodies of other forms and interesting new concepts.

The League of Gentlemen was written and performed by four talented young comedy actors. Initially performed as sketches at the Edinburgh Festival, *The League of Gentlemen* won the Perrier award in 1997. This led to the development of the horror/sitcom on BBC Radio 4 which then became the TV series on BBC2 (three series, 1999–2003).

Set in an eerie fictional Derbyshire town, the series was filled with strange characters and grisly secrets, evidently inspired by horror cinema. Interestingly, the structure changed for different series and introduced us to many different, strange characters even though there were generally the same four actors involved throughout.

Its elaborate and baroque style was matched by high production values. It was filmed on high-definition video tape with many outdoor shots and detailed sets, which is probably why it could move so easily on to cinema screens with the film *The League of Gentlemen's Apocalypse* being released in 2005 (earlier horror inspired sitcoms were *The Munsters* (1964–66) and *The Addams Family* (1964–66)).

There have been a variety of science-fiction/sitcom hybrids with *Mork & Mindy* (1978–82) and *Third Rock From The Sun* (1996–2001), both American productions that were also popular with British audiences. UK writers also produced the cult show *Red Dwarf*

(1988–99) and the more mainstream *My Hero*, first shown in February 2000. Using the sci-fi genre enables writers to look at the human condition truly from the viewpoint of an outsider. On the other hand it also allows audiences to laugh at the outsider without concerning themselves with political correctness; we don't have to worry about offending aliens.

It could also be valid to consider some police and hospital based sitcoms as hybrid genres. Though some are merely using the setting, programmes like *Scrubs* (2001–)incorporate aspects of the hospital drama and the sitcom format.

The comedy drama could be seen as a hybrid of the sitcom genre and drama but is generally thought of as a genre in its own right to describe programmes such as *Shameless* (2004–), *Sex and the City* (1998–2004), and *Skins*. The definition of comedy drama then seems to be comedy with a serious intent. Certainly the programmes cited as examples have more plot development and complex characters than your average sitcom; but the line between the sitcom and the comedy drama is sometimes a hazy one.

Structure

Taflinger devised a method of dividing situation comedies into three structured categories in his study 'Sitcom: What It Is, How It Works' (1996). These are the Actom, the Domcom and the Dramedy, and these are closely related to Aristotle's principles of drama – Action, Character and Thought.

The Actom

Taflinger defines the actcom as 'action focused comedy'. Here main characters are the protagonists in every plot. They are not complicated but they are leaders, and other characters serve only to follow them or be the one that suffers for the other's actions. The characters pay little heed to consequences. Taflinger suggests that in the actcom, plots are just there to make us laugh rather than make us think and there is no sense of a central theme or message.

The Domcom

Here the comedy is based around domestic issues. Themes are evident and mainly based around relationships. The main characters are keen to instil moral values in their children within stable families. They are more complex, with complicated motivations and are generally aware of consequences. Other characters may play an important role, with other family members being involved.

Character and thought are more important than action and common settings include middle-class homes.

The Dramedy

There are two different types of dramedy set out by Taflinger – the human dramedy and the advocate dramedy. What they share are plots centred on big issues and important messages. Characters are complex and plots follow how they cope with problems and difficulties associated with important themes, such as war or death.

In a human dramedy though, the characters are more likeable as they are more moderate and consider the plight of other people. They are intelligent and witty, and eventually they usually reach understanding. In the advocate dramedy, however, the central protagonist is usually selfish and assured of their superiority to other individuals. They are argumentative and rarely listen to others' points of view.

Though these definitions are helpful in the analysis of situation comedies, it is not always possible to neatly fit every sitcom in to a clear category. Some you may think contain elements from different types and even within one episode the style of sitcom can change as a particular theme or idea is explored.

Narrative structure

Typical elements of situation comedy include: a half-hour programme, usually as part of a short series; and a stand alone narrative so it is possible to appreciate the humour of each episode without viewing a whole series. Each week a new 'problem' causes humorous havoc, the comedy arising from the way in which the characters try and deal with this problem. The use of common situations such as home, family or work gives audiences familiar characters that they can identify with. And the use of small, regular casts, as in soap operas, also helps audiences to become familiar with the characters.

Sitcoms often follow the 'classic' narrative form, where the equilibrium is disrupted and each episode concludes with some sort of restoration to 'normality', depending on the style of the sitcom.

Action

The narrative action within a sitcom can have varying degrees of significance in relation to the exposition of humour. In some programmes the action centres on jokes rather than narrative structure, especially in programmes like *Bottom* (1991–95), that foreground slapstick humour rather than sophisticated development of plot. In other programmes there may not be much action at all, because the humour develops around the central character's reaction to their situation, as in *One Foot in the Grave* (1990–2000); or sometimes merely on their monologues on life, as in *Hancock* (1956–61) or *Shelley* (1979–92). The action of comedy narratives is centred around humorous situations and 'gags', which are the jokes built up to through the use of various comic strategies. Comic timing is an essential aspect of any gag, be it physical or verbal.

One classic form of structured plot in a sitcom is where actions and decisions lead to a build up of bizarre events that spiral out of control. Here everything ends in chaos so the equilibrium may not be restored. This kind of plot, where things go dramatically wrong for characters, can be seen in many sitcoms and often creates the climactic humour. In *The Young Ones* (1982–84), for example, Vivien was decapitated by a train in one episode, but he was back to normal for the following week.

Obviously, the style of the situation comedy that has been established directly impacts on the nature of bizarre events believable within that structure. *The Young Ones*, *Father Ted* (1995–98), *Red Dwarf* and *The IT Crowd* (2006–) are all only 'realistic' to a certain point and then they can go wherever the writers' imaginations want. The more domestic, 'realistic' style sitcoms like *My Family* (2000–), *Friends* (1994–2004) and *The Royle Family* (1998–2006) could not suddenly have a strange twist of events as it would totally disrupt the audience's expectations of that form.

Character

There are various character types that regularly appear in situation comedy: the nosy neighbour, the sexually voracious friend/relative, the loser. A common archetype is 'the fool', such as Baldrick from *Blackadder* (1983–89), and 'the foil', the opposite of the central character who is often 'the straight man'. These character types remind us of very early stage comedy. In commedia dell'arte and even Roman theatre, stock characters were important to comedy plays.

Character and performance are an enormously important part of situation comedy, as often the programme may be entirely built around the reputation of the lead actor. Some sitcoms have been developed around characters who appeared in sketch shows, such as *Knowing Me Knowing You...with Alan Partridge* (1994–95). Others have been designed to showcase a comedian's techniques rather than develop character, such as *Terry and Julian* (1992), starring Julian Clarey as 'himself' but in a situation comedy structure. Other sitcoms' success seems to be largely defined by the performance of the central actor. For example, though David Jason was not the original choice for Del Boy in *Only Fools and Horses* (1981–2003), it is now hard to imagine the character being played by anyone else. Also, central characters in British sitcoms are often fatally flawed and we are invited to laugh at them rather than with them.

Verbal humour

In British situation comedy in particular, the dialogue between characters can be a crucial part of a programme's pleasure. Verbal wit is an important aspect of dialogue in many situation comedies and comic timing is essential for this to work effectively for audiences. The sarcastic remark has to come straight after the mistake for it to hit audiences before they think of the funny retort themselves.

Sarcasm and wit are often major features of comedy performance. Tony Hancock, John Cleese and Richard Wilson could go on for hours with huge ranting sarcastic speeches which audiences gain great pleasure from, monologues being a large aspect of verbal humour too. Dialogue often involves the delivery of jokes, but can also establish the relationship between characters which may be an important aspect of the humour in a programme.

Satire includes parody and often sarcasm. It is one of the earliest forms of humour, used in Greek and Roman theatre and even then it was associated with mocking politicians. Satire usually mocks people with wealth and power. *Yes Minister* (1980–84) and *The New Statesman* (1987–94) are good examples of satirical sitcoms that proved very popular. Interestingly, *Yes Minister/Prime Minister* (1986–88) was enjoyed by politicians even though it mocked the systems of Parliament and political dodgy dealing. Mrs Thatcher was reported to enjoy the humour and realism of the programme, which won three BAFTA awards in annual succession.

Satire, though, is not especially associated with situation comedy, perhaps because it can be difficult to sustain in realistic narratives, which are more common in this comedy form. It is more prevalent in sketch shows based on comedy impressionists or stand-up comedians, such as *Bremner, Bird and Fortune* (1999–) and the revered *Spitting Image* (1984–96).

Verbal wit is a big part of satire and plays a notable role in many British situation comedies in particular. Wit is the oral realisation of humour, including puns and jokes. This wit might be used to mock other characters, sometimes quite mercilessly as in *Blackadder*, or to generally rail against the unfairness of humanity like Basil Fawlty in *Fawlty Towers* (1975–79) or Victor Meldrew in *One Foot in the Grave*. Wordplay, irony and wit are important aspects of British humour, perhaps due to our literary heritage. Puns and playing around with language seem to have always been popular with British audiences if we consider writers such as Chaucer and Shakespeare.

Black humour, like satire, can cause controversy because here serious situations like death and illness are observed and then undermined for comic effect. *Six Feet Under* (2001–05) and *Desperate Housewives* (2004–) are good examples of comedy dramas that use this style but *M*A*S*H* (1972–83), an American sitcom set in an army hospital in the Korean War, is an excellent example of a sitcom predicated upon black humour. It also displayed a lot of wit and sometimes verged on slapstick, but underlying all this was the horrific background of a war hospital where doctors would heal young men just so they could be sent back to risk their lives again.

Catchphrases are the repetition of certain phrases, spoken on a regular basis. They are used primarily to stick in our minds and are a common characteristic of comedy shows and sometime sitcoms, such as Jim Royle's 'My arse' in *The Royle Family* and Victor Meldrew's 'I don't believe it!' in *One Foot in the Grave*.

These are almost like advertising slogans in that they remind us of our favourite characters and, therefore, our favourite programmes, when we hear other people repeating them in our everyday lives. Catchphrases are usually associated with one particular character and are one of the audience pleasures of the comedy form.

Visual humour

Slapstick and ludicrous situations have been common since the early days of sitcom, a popular form left over from the vaudeville and the silent comedy films.

Physical violence and comic timing are the keys aspects of slapstick, and though many situation comedies feature snapshots of physical humour only a few modern programmes feature it as their main source of comedy. Good examples would be *The Young Ones* and *Bottom*, which both starred Ade Edmondson and Rik Mayall. Michael Crawford also celebrated the form with *Some Mothers Do 'Ave 'Em* (1973–78).

Some comedy actors are renowned for their ability to use facial expressions and their body language to create comedy. For example,

John Cleese's manic expressions and physical movement are a huge part of what we enjoy to watch in his performance as Basil Fawlty. Rowan Atkinson was nicknamed 'rubber face' and Lee Evans also has a similar ability to contort his face to amuse audiences with exaggerated facial expressions.

But visual humour does not just relate to the performers, but also to aspects of the set, costume and comic moments in the plot: For example, the living room on *Father Ted*, when Father Jack is contained in a plastic bubble so as to cause less offence; the elaborate clothing of Patsy and Eddie in *Absolutely Fabulous* (1992–2005); and the apartment where Del and Rodney live in *Only Fools and Horses*.

Form

Another interesting element to observe in sitcom is the number of main characters the plot revolves around, as this makes a difference to other technical aspects. There are three basic structures:

1. A comedy partnership where the humour is developed around the relationship between two main characters. Similarly to police drama 'partners', these characters are often in conflict with each other for some reason. They may have very different personalities or different beliefs and desires, for example. But something keeps them together – they may be related or they might just not have anyone else that will put up with them.

2. Sitcoms based around the relationships and actions of a group of characters, with no single protagonist being solely responsible for the humour. Each character will have some trait that distinguishes them from the others. This kind of comedy has the added attraction of socialisation, as audiences can compare themselves to characters in the programme.

3. In a number of situation comedies, although there may be important catalytic characters, generally one character is the central protagonist throughout the series. These characters often feel superior to the people around them and have great ambitions and dreams that they will go on to achieve higher things. The humour usually centres on them trying to achieve these dreams – and failing.

There is often an underlying tension in the sitcom which is important to the narrative. Conflict is important, as in all drama, but here it is used to create humour rather than serious problems. Part of the pleasure for audiences is predicting how the main characters will deal with these situations. Their familiarity with these characters allows the audience to enjoy the anticipation, as well as the realisation of the humour.

Predictability is often part of the enjoyment of a situation comedy. We can predict that Basil Fawlty of *Fawlty Towers* will, at some point in the programme, lose his temper and behave outrageously. We can predict that Blackadder will hit Baldrick and we can predict Del Boy will call Rodney a 'plonker'. Certain patterns of behaviour or even catchphrases are the elements sitcoms used to ensure audiences tune in to a full series.

Setting

The two most common settings for situation comedy are the home and the workplace; but even when not set in either of these two places they are usually set around some sort of community. This is because it is the interaction of familiar characters and their relationships with each other that are often the source of the humour.

The workplace

Situation comedies set in the workplace could be compared to their dramatic counterparts as there are probably more drama series set around the workplace than comedies; perhaps because not enough people associate their jobs with fun! And the range of workplaces and jobs featured in sitcoms include dinner ladies, funeral directors, the police force, hospitals, sewing factories and rag and bone men.

Of course, we all have different jobs but within the workplace we all have similar disagreements with colleagues, annoying bosses and strange work mates. Situation comedies based in the workplace will, similarly to dramas, portray characters with strong, clashing personalities, characters having illicit affairs and characters who are just bored with their job. But the sitcom will further exaggerate these relationships and put them into awkward situations to make them funny, as in *Scrubs*, or add bizarre characters, as in *The Green Wing* (2004–).

The other good practical reason for setting a situation comedy in the workplace is that if an actor wants to move on you can replace them with someone else quite legitimately without audiences having to suspend their disbelief further at the sight of a new actor playing a similar character out of the blue. For example, the long running *Cheers* (1982–93) saw two major changes in actors: 'The Coach' (Nicholas Colasanto) was replaced by 'Woody' (Woody Harrelson), not as a change in actor but as a new character who had been trained by the Coach, through the mail, to work behind the bar; and Manager Diane (Shelly Long) was replaced with Rebecca, played by Kirstie Alley. In both cases the new characters were easily intergrated and audiences could feel reassured by as they got used to them.

The domestic setting

The domestic setting used in situation comedy can be compared to the setting of the soap opera, as the drama revolves around family and community life. These kinds of setting are so common because they are within almost everybody's range of experiences. Many popular situation comedies have been established around the family home; the comedy revolving around the common clashes between parents and their offspring, and the parents with each other. There have been so many shows based around the family that it might be considered to be an overdone premise for a situation comedy, but it may be the latter day mediocrity of these programmes rather than the narrative premise that has lessened their impact. However, there have been relatively recent family-based sitcoms that have made an impact, especially *Roseanne* (1988–97) and *The Royle Family*, where the representation of the working-class family is more realistic than idealistic.

The role of women within the family has been an issue in situation comedies since *I Love Lucy* (1951–60), with women often being seen as the more sensible or intelligent partner, even though they may have a subordinate role to the man. It is interesting though, that there have been relatively few sitcoms that dealt with split families, considering the high divorce rate in modern times. This could bring up discussions with your students regarding ideology and social values, and why some contemporary issues seem to be dealt with in comedy but others aren't.

2. Generations of Comedy

It is always interesting to consider the historical development of a genre and compare programmes we enjoyed in the past with those we enjoy now. In Media Studies this can also be an interesting aspect of classwork, but probably the most significant approach to sitcoms of the past is to consider what they tell us about social and cultural aspects of the times in which they were created. In fact it would be difficult to ignore these elements with students as changes in the representation of various groups is often very noticeable, especially relating to gender and race. What was acceptable to make jokes about in the 1970s is not so for modern audiences. In terms of the form itself, the structure of the sitcom has changed very little but *styles* have and this could also be a significant aspect to discuss with students.

So while Chapter 2 briefly considers the situation comedy since the 1950s up to the present day, it also looks at one or two examples of situation comedies that stood out in these decades. Their significance may be cultural, due to popularity, or because they challenged audiences at the time; but hopefully they will all offer a starting point for developing work on situation comedy.

Radio and the 1950s

Situation comedy is an established form in television and has been since the very early days of broadcasting. As with many television genres situation comedies originated on the radio and some of the stars of radio comedy were originally stars from variety entertainment and vaudeville. There were three main BBC radio stations in the 1950s: the Light Programme, the Third Programme and the Home Service. Of these, the Light Programme is most associated with variety shows and comedy.

The early radio comedy programmes were shows based on the vaudeville shows that had previously been successful in the theatre, with many of the stars attempting to directly transfer their comedy performances and skills from the stage to the radio studio. Thus early programmes were based around sketches and songs rather than narratives. This kind of humour was often rather 'visual' for radio, so it was only a matter of time before new styles needed to develop. Thus, sketch shows and humorous characters were developed, and so the first situation comedies were established.

Not all radio comedy actors made a successful leap from the stage to the radio and this is quite understandable. Actors, especially comedy actors, often rely on the relationship they have with their live audience – the laughter encouraging them to take their act that one step further, the applause the motivator of their antics.

A lot of stage comedy focused on physical humour such as slapstick and the kind of 'he's behind you' humour we enjoy today in pantomime. This humour does not move smoothly from the stage to the radio, which is not to say visual or physical humour cannot exist on the radio. *The Goon Show* (1951–60), for example, prided itself on the antics it performed on radio. Their surreal style of comedy would have been difficult to perform on television in the 1950s but with the help of a vivid imagination, it was an extremely popular radio show.

There are a number of early comic radio shows that played an important part in the development of the situation comedy form. *Sam and Henry*, which later became *Amos and Andy* on television (1951–53), was seen by some to be the first situation comedy on American radio. Aired between 1926 and 1927 it was inspired by Sidney Smith's popular comic strip *The Gumps* but the writers, Charles Correll and Freeman Gosden, created their own characters based on these earlier characters. Correll and Gosden were both white but they played black characters, a lot of the humour being based around their strong accents and stereotypical representations of 'negroes', popular with American audiences at this time.

Radio comedy seemed to be particularly successful for comedy duos and this continued with Burns and Allen, Fibber McGee and Molly, and Vic and Sadie.

Band Waggon (1938–40) starred Arthur Askey and Richard Murdoch, and though the show was initially made up of a series of jokes, its continuity led to the development of humour relating to situations. The show was based around two comedians who live in a flat on the roof of BBC Broadcasting House. It included regular characters and catchphrases, as many situation comedies do today.

It's That Man Again (ITMA) was a popular wartime radio comedy. The title initially referred to Adolf Hitler and the programme centred on mocking Hitler and Nazi propaganda in general. The show ran for ten years from 1939–49 and was built around it's star, Tommy Handley, playing a town mayor. For one season in 1941 it was called *It's That Sand Again*, but reverted to its original title and didn't finish until the death of its star in 1949.

Ray's a Laugh centred around comedian Ted Ray, and his fictional jobs at the Cannon Enquiry Agency and later *The Daily Bugle* as a reporter. Focusing on Ted's work and home life, and including many catchphrases, the programme had an important role to play in the development of the situation comedy. *Ray's a Laugh* ran from 1949–61.

Take It From Here, ran from 1948–58 and brought together the writing talents of Frank Muir and Denis Norden. *TIFH* was more of a sketch show than a situation comedy, though it had a regular setting (a radio station), and a family called 'The Glums' were introduced to the show in the 1950s. The Glums later received their own series.

Life With The Lyons was an interesting show in terms of the development of sitcoms, as it centred on a real life family. The scripts, written by the mother of the family – Bebe Daniels – were based on real life events that were then exaggerated for humorous effect. The show also included Ben Lyon (Daniels' husband); Richard and Barbara, the two children, a housekeeper, nosy neighbour and even the family dog, Skeeter. The show began in 1950 and went on to become a successful television show and was made into several films.

In Britain, comedy was an important part of the scheduling from radio's very early days. *Hancock's Half Hour* is generally accepted as the first British situation comedy as we now recognise it and its format has been the model for many modern sitcoms ever since (see below).

Many British comedy programmes, writers and stars on television were first heard on BBC radio. Programmes such as *Knowing Me, Knowing You... with Alan Partridge* and *The League of Gentlemen* followed in the footsteps of *Hancock's Half Hour* by starting their lives on the radio before becoming successful on television.

It is evident that radio has been instrumental in the development of the situation comedy as we know it on our television screens today. Radio was where the form began, rising out of the vaudeville style sketch shows, evolving into comedy set around a regular situation and set of characters. As early radio made stars of Peter Sellers, Frank Muir and Tony Hancock, so radio has continued to be an important stepping stone for contemporary comedy stars.

However, the role of comedy on radio has changed with the advent of digital television. Up-and-coming comedy writers and actors can now sidestep radio and go straight to television, using BBC3 as their first step into television comedy. This doesn't mean there is no comedy on the radio anymore though. Some comedians continue with radio work alongside their television work. Radio 4 and 2 still broadcast popular radio comedy shows and BBC Radio 7 specialises in comedy shows.

Case Study: *Hancock's Half Hour*

Hancock's Half Hour

Hancock's Half Hour is still considered one of the most important British situation comedies of all times and it was first broadcast on the radio in 1954. The television show based on this radio programme began in 1956 through a previous sketch show bearing Hancock's name.

Generally, *Hancock's Half Hour* focused on the complaints and frustrations of Tony Hancock (the character and actor). Though the comedy centred on the character of Hancock, Sid James regularly co-starred as Hancock's right hand man and other actors well known in comedy worked with him less regularly, including Kenneth Williams and Hattie Jaques who went on to dominate the *Carry On* films.

Sketch and variety shows were still the most dominant forms in radio at the time and the writers of *Hancock's Half Hour* wanted to move away from this. Hancock, too, was keen to show snippets of everyday life and portray an insight into the human psyche. The programme considered the relationships between the characters and the situations they found themselves in, marking the beginning of the style of British sitcom that has continued to dominate television.

The setting was mainly Hancock's home, his address often being quoted in the show and so becoming one of the most famous comedy addresses (23 Railway Cuttings, East Cheam). The radio programme was developed into a television sitcom in 1956 and still involved the same writers (Roy Galton and Alan Simpson) but not all of the same actors. The radio show continued to run alongside the successful TV show for another three years and was still popular with audiences, even though they could now see their favourite character on new-fangled television.

Tony Hancock created the pompous and frustrated character that is a classic representation of comedy and drama – the ambitious anti-hero. Like a lot of Greek and Shakespearian characters before him, and many a situation comedy central character after him, Anthony Aloysius St John Hancock thought he should be a lot more successful in the world than he actually was. He was irritated easily, bored often and wasn't a very likeable person. But Hancock the actor had natural comic talent which did not merely develop from the excellent scripts. He had a natural wit, a talent for mimicry and exaggerated facial expressions. His fast delivery and excellent comic timing meant he occasionally still produced excellent shows when he didn't know his lines. Hancock was not frightened of using pauses for comic effect, a difficult element to get right, particularly when the show was only on the radio.

Realism, verbal wit and sarcasm have since been important elements of many British situation comedies with numerous writers and comedy actors alike quoting the Hancock series as a major influence on them. This is not to say that all British sitcoms are social realist in their style, but there is a tendency in British situation comedy (which is not true of a lot of American comedies) to show human beings with major flaws who have no desire to see the error of their ways. This kind of character is a common form in situation comedy that we will look at in further detail lin Chapter 4. We don't often like these characters and we are invited to laugh *at* them not with them, largely because of their many personality flaws.

The 1960s

Changes in society in the 1960s had a major influence on the situation comedy form, largely in relation to social class. Opportunities in education and the increased mobility of the working class meant writers and artists from these backgrounds were gaining a social voice. And they wanted to portray narratives and characters from their traditions and backgrounds. Writers like John Osborne and Keith Waterhouse and film-makers like Ken

Loach had something to say about working class life. It was therefore only a matter of time until social class became a topic in situation comedy.

In the 1960s there were around 100 situation comedies on British television. Most of these were original ideas rather than being based on earlier radio shows and as the establishment censors were becoming more lenient, writers and producers were developing wider ranges of characters and ideas. As more situation comedies were portraying working class lives, this led to workplace settings showing realistic snapshots of the lifestyle and humour in everyday situations.

The Rag Trade (1961–63), for example, was a popular workplace-based situation comedy of this era, set in a sewing factory in the East End of London. The same writers, Ronald Wolfe and Ronald Chesney, went on to devise *On the Buses* (1969–73) and although that was just a few years later, these shows were very different in their approach to comedy in the workplace. *The Rag Trade* represented working women who had strong opinions and plenty to say about their working and personal lives. This challenged conventional representation at this time but was still very popular. The show's representation of working class women as strong and intelligent was not like any other contemporary situation comedy; the women had all the best lines. It seems disappointing to follow this with *On the Buses* which focused on the adventures of Stan Butler and Jack Harper with women playing the roles of hideous nags or sexual playthings.

But as the 70s were fast approaching, the sexual revolution was taking a different direction. *On the Buses* was all about sexual innuendo and mischief as the two friends cavorted with beautiful 'clippies' and generally infuriated their boss, Blakey. The *Carry On* films were also popular at this time, reflecting a change in society's attitude towards sex. Sex was now about freedom, not fear. There was so much fast-moving social and cultural change in the 1960s and situation comedy of the time reflected both the old and the new social values.

Probably the most significant sitcom of the 1960s was *Till Death Us Do Part* (1966–75), starring Warren Mitchell as the controversial character Alf Garnett. Its importance is due to various reasons, the simplest of these being its popularity. The show ran for ten years and produced a successful American spin-off, *All in the Family* (1971–79), as well as two feature films. Another reason for its impact is its style. It was one of the first situation comedies to adopt the style of the 'kitchen sink' dramas, showing a working class family, often in conflict with each other, who struggled financially. Alf Garnett was an opinionated and intolerant working class Conservative who loved the Queen and hated immigrants. His son-in-law was a Liverpuddlian socialist, the antithesis of Alf.

This programme clearly portrayed the generation gap that was so noticeable at this time. But the main thing *Till Death Us Do Part* will be remembered for is the debate creator Johnny Speight sparked via his creation. Alf Garnett's opinions were neither the actor's nor the writer's but not all audiences saw the irony and this caused issue with many critics. The *Radio Times* said: 'If you laugh with Alf Garnett you have merely been entertained. If you laugh at him you have been entertained and informed – and that's a victory for Johnny Speight' (bbc.co.uk, Guide to Comedy).

The 1970s

In the 1970s society was still enjoying the social revolution that started in the 60s. More people were upwardly mobile, were living together outside wedlock and committing to inter-racial relationships to challenge social norms. Some situation comedies, such as *Mixed Blessings* (1978–80), attempted to deal with these issues and though they could be accused of showing a lack of sensitivity and depth, there were some programmes around in the 70s that did make interesting social comments.

It is possible to consider the 1970s as a time in which political correctness was non-existent. Programmes like *Love Thy Neighbour* (1972–76) and *It Ain't Half Hot Mum* (1974–81) portrayed simplistic and stereotypical representations of ethnic groups at a time when Britain was nurturing a multi-cultural society. *Mind Your Language* (1977–79) was intended to represent this society by portraying an English language school, but it was filled with one dimensional, stereotypical representations of people from many different countries, such as Italy, Pakistan and Sweden. Of course, the teacher was British and *his* representation was entirely different.

Watching these retrospectively they seem shockingly simplistic and sometimes offensive, but it is important to consider historical context. Britain was only just emerging as a multi-cultural nation and this was met with differing reactions. British writers' intentions may have been good, but some of the jokes and characters we see in sitcoms at this time reflect what was largely acceptable then, not now, and should be studied with that clearly in mind.

Other programmes represented different changes in Britain's

society. Probably the most interesting representation in 70s sitcoms was a middle class disillusioned by their semi-detached suburbia. *The Good Life* (1975–78), *The Rise and Fall of Reginald Perrin* (1976–79) and *Butterflies* (1978–82) all had this cynicism at their heart, even though they expressed it in quite different ways. *The Good Life* may have been a rather twee representation of a suburban couple seeking an idealised self-sufficient life while maintaining their middle class home, but *Reginald Perrin* and *Butterflies* were not quite as sunny in outlook.

The 1980s

The Young Ones

A new generation of comedies in the 1980s seemed to reflect the rebellion of the punk era that began in the late 70s. Comedians following the likes of Bernard Manning and Jimmy Tarbuck decided they wanted a new comedy club that would reflect their new aspirations. The Comic Strip Club was opened in 1980 by Peter Richardson, and was the place where practically the whole cast of *The Young Ones* honed their comedy craft. The situation comedy was considered to be part of the establishment at this time and the alternative comedians were generally performing stand-up on programmes such as *Friday Night Live* (1988).

But even alternative comedians can exploit the form of situation comedy and *The Young Ones* became the first 'alternative' sitcom. The programme was based on anarchic, slapstick and violent humour, with surreal elements and a musical interlude, similar to the early radio sitcoms. The basic structure of the programme was a typical situation comedy – a half hour format in a short series with an ensemble cast of very different characters with a fractious relationship with each other.

New wave, alternative comedy was established through the popularity of *The Young Ones* and the big names of comedy and comedy writing that are still popular today made their mark.

The 1980s was all about extremes. The South had 'yuppies' and the North was struggling with high unemployment as key industries like mining were closing down, effecting whole communities. Stand-up comedians like Ben Elton and Harry Enfield explicitly criticised Tory policy, but only a few situation comedies took a stand.

Another alternative comedian who went on to establish himself in the situation comedy form was Rowan Atkinson. The *Blackadder* series ran throughout the 1980s and beyond with Atkinson co-writing and starring in this long running, popular programme.

Probably the most endearing and popular sitcom to be produced in the 1980s is *Only Fools and Horses*. It is still regarded as one of the most popular, contemporary situation comedies, yet it is now a decade since the last series was produced. It made a star of David Jason who had only played supporting comedy roles up to then, yet the series nearly didn't get past the first two series because of poor viewing figures.

Case Study: *Only Fools and Horses*

John Sullivan was determined to become a comedy writer, even though he'd had little formal education. He was working moving sets at the BBC and was for a time employed on the set of *Porridge* (1974–77). Sullivan's break came when he managed to give some sketches he'd written to the star Ronnie Barker, who used them on *The Two Ronnies* (1971–87). Writing *Citizen Smith* (1977–79) then established his reputation and he went on to write *Only Fools and Horses*.

Roy Butt, the producer of *Only Fools and Horses*, was from the same sort of working class London background as John Sullivan, and creating an accurate representation of this background was important to both of them in the early programmes. This was evident in the representation of social issues and culture prevalent throughout the series.

Luck was on Sullivan's side when it came to the production of a new series as initial viewing figures were not high and the programme was nearly dropped. The main reason a third series was commissioned, even without the viewing figures, was due to the BBC

Only Fools and Horses

apparently not having anything sufficiently well advanced to replace it with. There was also a dispute which led to *Only Fools* changing its place in the schedule, which meant a larger audience could be targeted and the programme changed from 30 minutes to 50 minutes. Sullivan began to further develop the characters and his own skills for writing female roles after writing the romantic comedy, *Just Good Friends* (1983–86). It wasn't long after this that two strong, female characters were written in to *Only Fools and Horses*.

Only Fools and Horses had a very strong narrative thread running through the series and reflected the society and culture of the 1980s. Del wanted to be a Yuppie and Rodney worried about nuclear war. Though audiences may have been laughing at Del trying desperately to be part of a culture he would always remain apart from, Sullivan was also clearly making a point about society at the time. Rodney had principles and Del just wanted to make money. Their characters reflected the two opposing sides to the 1980s. But the brotherly love that existed between them was undeniable and definitely one of the draws of this sitcom. All sitcoms based on partnerships need a reason the two stay together and that they are brothers is theirs. This might not be seen as enough for some, but the importance of family is an important aspect of working class culture, something that can also be observed in soaps like *EastEnders* (1985–) and *Coronation Street* (1960–).

Throughout the programmes, the *mise-en-scène* of the flat in Nelson Mandela house was an important aspect of the comedy. The cocktail bar, wallpaper, boxes overflowing with dodgy goods, were all important parts of the programme's appeal. Twenty-five million viewers tuned into the 1996 Christmas special where the boys did indeed become millionaires, smashing all previous records for a comedy programme.

The 90s and beyond

There have been significant changes in the television industry and the situation comedy genre in this time period which has led some to suggest the age of the sitcom has passed. Though the 90s and 2000s have produced some significant situation comedies, programmes are not achieving the same kind of audience ratings as they once did in part because of the proliferation of digital channels. Situation comedies used to be a large part of mainstream channels' scheduling, designed to reach and be enjoyed by large, family audiences. But now writers are targeting smaller audiences and sitcoms tend to be commissioned for BBC2 and Channel 4, if not the specialist digital channels dedicated to comedy or youth progamming, such as BBC3.

In some ways this is a good thing. This period has seen some of the most experimental and sophisticated comedy for years. Programmes like *The Office* (2001–03), with its clever use of documentary techniques, speak directly to audiences in a time when reality TV saturates the schedule. Also, there have been a range of animated sitcoms aimed at adults throughout this time. Starting with *The Simpsons* (1989–), the US has continued to create these dry portrayals of family life, often with an additional bizarre edge, only possible within the work of animation, e.g. *King of the Hill* (1997–).

There have been very popular long-running sitcoms that have captured elements of contemporary living in this era, namely *Friends* and *Seinfeld* (1989–98). There was also *Sex and the City*, which, though not a sitcom as such, certainly had comparable elements and discussed aspects of 90s American culture using humour.

Comedy shows in Britain at this time such as *The Vicar of Dibley* (1994–2007) and *One Foot in the Grave*, broadcast on BBC1, were definitely popular with mainstream audiences. Both programmes reflected life in the 90s in their own way. *The Vicar of Dibley*, though quite gentle and simplistic in its plots and characterisation, did deal with the issue of female ordination when it was still a controversial issue. *One Foot in the Grave* was a black comedy which followed the self-inflicted misery of Victor Meldrew as he railed against the idiosyncrasies of modern living.

Contemporary sitcoms seem to be moving away from the traditional production of the form: the three camera set-up, studio audience and laughter track. But there remain writers like Graham Linehan who, with *The IT Crowd* in 2006, are happy to continue to use traditional techniques. There are sitcoms being produced that are intelligent and experimental, which is important and positive; but the lack of successful mainstream sitcoms is noticeable and must inform us about the needs and desires of modern TV audiences.

The development of American situation comedy

Situation comedy started on television in the US before the UK and one of the early popular shows was *Father Knows Best* (1954–60). This sitcom portrayed the epitome of the perfect American family. Morally and socially upstanding they lived in Springfield, no doubt ironically used by Groening in *The Simpsons*. The representations were stereotypical: she was the all-American mom and he was the hard working dad. The children were well behaved and the programme was heavily into promoting the perfect lifestyle.

This programme was a huge contrast to *I Love Lucy* which was produced in 1951. A very successful and popular series, that was big in the UK as well as the US, it was very influential if not the starting point for other sitcoms to follow. *I Love Lucy* portrayed a real life husband and wife team (Desi Arnaz and Lucille Ball) representing Lucy as a rebellious housewife who longs to be in show business.

Her husband, of course, thinks a woman's place is in the home and most of the humour centres on her attempts to escape the confines of her position. It could be suggested that her rebellious acts exposed the restrictions of women at the time. Lucy wanted to make her own money and follow her ambitions – but whenever she tried to by taking a job, or performing at the club where her husband worked as a musician, it always ended in a humorous disaster.

One preferred reading of this is that women should know their place; but the flip side to this sitcom is the real life aspect of the show. Lucille Ball was a very popular, successful comedy actress who was asked to do this show. It was originally designed for her and another actor but she insisted that her real life husband Arnaz play the role of Ricky. This dynamic adds a different edge to the show. In real life Desi Arnaz was a successful musician but not the star that Lucille Ball was, and it is her irrepressible energy as a performer that undermines the message of the half-hearted resolution when she goes back to being a housewife. You know she can never be contained!

Other early American situation comedies on television also had political and social comments to make. Though they may seem quite simplistic in terms of their narratives and character representation, *The Beverly Hillbillies* (1962–71) and *The Munsters* made some interesting points about American social values.

The Beverly Hillbillies showed a family of simple country folk moving to Beverly hills when they make it rich. Commenting on the increased mobility of the working class and the snobbery this instigates, *The Beverly Hillbillies* succeed in undermining the constraints of middle class life. *The Beverly Hillbillies* was a very popular show, running from 1962–71 on CBS. In fact, it was only due to advertisers not reaching the preferred demographic for their products that led to the show being pulled, as audience ratings remained high to the end. The show was repeated in the UK on Channel 4 in the late 80s/early 90s.

The Munsters was another American classic that was repeated on UK screens in the 80s. They were a caring and loving American family. Morally and socially upstanding, the family fulfilled their responsibilities to each other with pride. Herman, the head of the household was keen to be the best husband and father he could and Lillian, his wife, adored him. They represented the ideal American family. The twist was that all the family members were based on classic horror characters. Herman was Frankenstein's monster; Lillian his bride and Grandpa was a vampire who longed for life in 'the old country'.

Though they frightened everyone that came across them, it was *The Munsters* that were the 'good guys', as their innocence and openness often got them into situations where unscrupulous characters would try and take advantage of them; especially Marilyn, the misfit in the family, who is in fact the beautiful 'normal' one.

Misunderstandings and miscreants created a gentle, light-hearted humour but at the heart of *The Munsters* there seems to be a comment about American society. Fear of the unknown and assumptions about anyone who is 'different' have caused political problems in America in the past (and the present) and was an issue at the heart of *The Munsters*.

In the late 60s music played an increasingly important part in young people's lives and American writers were quick to see the benefits of fitting popular music into the sitcom genre. *The Partridge Family* (1970–74) and *The Monkees* (1966–68) used music as part of their format, but still maintained a situation comedy structure.

But there have been other programmes, like *M*A*S*H*, that were designed to make American audiences sit up and think. An extremely popular sitcom, *M*A*S*H* ran from the early 70s until the late 80s. Based on the successful film directed by Robert Altman, the series followed the day to day horror of working in a military hospital during the Korean War. Not an obvious place to set a sitcom, but the humour centred on the wit and mischievousness of two doctors who used their humour as a coping mechanism. The series had plenty to say about the futility of war and though it was set in Korea, it clearly referred to the Vietnam War that American soldiers were involved in when the series began. The production values of the programme reflected the earlier film as it was shot on film rather than video and lots of filming took place on location, which was, and still is, unusual in the sitcom genre.

Amongst the more moralising and idealist domestic sitcoms, there were still those that challenged expectations being released during the 1980s. *The Wonder Years* (1988–93) was a feel-good, retrospective situation comedy that charted the transition from childhood through adolescence of Kevin Arnold. Narrated by the adult Kevin, it was set in the late 60s/early 70s reflecting social issues and the challenges of growing up at this time. Shot on film *The Wonder Years* combined classic music of the era with a depth of understanding of relationships to create a memorable sitcom.

Comedy films

To fully explore the situation comedy form it is important to consider developments within film comedy, in addition to that of the radio and theatre comedy forms previously discussed. The earliest comedy films centred on slapstick, as the films were short and silent. Narratives were very simple, if they existed and similarly to radio, were often based on routines audiences were used to seeing at the theatre.

As film technology developed so did the film narratives and instead of the storyline developing from the humour, the humour developed more naturally from the narrative. However, famous comedy actors such as Buster Keaton and Harold Lloyd were so important to the humour of the films they were in because it was their personna that inspired much of the comedy. It was the stars audiences flocked to see rather than the films themselves.

The elements important to comedy films are also important to situation comedy. Performance-centred comedy is an important aspect of many films, and well known comedy actors such as John Cleese, Ronnie Barker and Tony Hancock have made their mark on the sitcom genre just as the likes of Stan Laurel and Oliver Hardy did in comedy films. Comic film actors are also often cited as important influences on the success of modern day comedians who look back on early comedy stars such as the Marx Brothers and Chaplin as their earliest inspirations.

There are also similarities in the narratives of some films and situation comedies, with physical gags and outrageous plot outcomes being just as popular in the *Home Alone* films (1990, 1992, 1997) and Charlie Chaplin films as is such sitcoms as *The IT Crowd* or *Gimme, Gimme, Gimme* (1999–2001).

The Ealing comedies and *Carry On* films also have an important role in the history of comedy, particularly reflecting the British approach to humour. Ealing studios opened in 1931 but it was just after the Second World War that they began to create comedy films with a particular style that became their trademark. The Ealing comedies reflected a nation in transition. They showed a dislike for austerity and promoted a sense of togetherness and loyalty. These films also often displayed a sentimental attitude to the past which is also an element that helps to popularise certain television programmes today.

It is clear why this kind of comedy would be popular in post-war Britain and this kind of humour is still popular in British situation comedy now. Consider the long-running success of *The Last of the Summer Wine* (1973–) and programmes such as *Hi-De-Hi!* (1980–88). Older audiences, in particular, like to be reminded of the good things from their past and enjoy remembering their youth.

Another interesting success story in British film-making is the *Carry On* films. Pinewood studios created 31 *Carry On* films over a 20 year period. *Carry On* films are all about puns, double entendres and general naughtiness. They mocked British attitudes towards sex, British institutions and history from 1958–78. These cheaply produced films were hugely popular and still are today after numerous TV repeats throughout the years.

In television this kind of mockery of institutions can be observed in situation comedy such as *Yes Minister* and historical periods are an important aspect of the *Blackadder* series. It is also clear from continuing comedies that puns and rude jokes are still popular with audiences, for example, in the episode of *Phoenix Nights* (2001–02) when Brian Potter accidentally hires an inflatable castle designed for a more adult audience for a children's party.

Comedy films are probably the most popular genre amongst teenage audiences so it could be interesting to compare their film viewing and situation comedy viewing experiences. When we look at modern day films we see many similarities to situation comedies because comic strategies and good comedy actors are the key aspects to successful comedy.

3. Comic Strategies

There are many different situation comedies covering a wide range of settings, people and types of humour, which may sometimes make it difficult to actually identify a situation comedy. A group of people on a futuristic space ship, a group of Catholic priests in Ireland and a deranged bookshop proprietor are all the basis of recent situation comedies (*Red Dwarf*, *Father Ted* and *Black Books* (2000–04), respectively), but all offer very different situations and different expositions of the humour. However, elements such as comic surprise or suspense and central characters with eccentric personality traits will be used no matter where a sitcom is set.

In Chapter 11 I outlined the comic strategies common to all comic forms, be it variety, drama or stand up. In this section I am going to focus on how comic strategies are used in situation comedies and go into more detail on how strategies are implemented in some particular performances. This is quite a difficult area to cover with students, as it is where we attempt to define and deconstruct the technicalities of comedy and there is no exact terminology agreed on by scholars with which to do this.

First, 'humour' and 'comedy' are terms I use frequently in this *Guide* – but the meanings attached to these terms are slightly different. Basically, it's all about intention. We may find a situation or story funny, but it is only comedy if it was *intended* to be funny.

Also, it is important to consider the construction of comedy moments within the situation comedy genre. The joke is the simplest and smallest component of comedy and though not necessarily the main aspect of the humour within sitcoms, it remains an important aspect. We generally consider jokes to be the short quip, with a subject, set-up and punch line. They are mostly used by stand up comedians, and shared in playgrounds and workplaces. Jokes might involve stereotypes, puns and even physical aspects so in some ways they involve all comic strategies in miniature. As in all comic forms, the social sharing of a joke or the isolation of the people the joke is about is an important aspect of the humour.

There are various different types of joke and gag and analysing these varied structures would be important if looking at comedy as a whole; but in the study of sitcoms it is probably more significant to look at the way a joke is set up and realised within an episode. Certainly, though, jokes offer teachers an attention-grabbing, easy way in to discussing many areas relevant to situation comedy – such as stereotypes, representation and comic timing. In some ways, I would suggest an episode of a situation comedy can act like a giant joke: it has the subject, the character(s), the build up and then the climactic ending as the punchline.

The two main styles of comedy are basically physical or verbal, but within this there are many layers of possible comedic realisation. As discussed earlier, verbal comedy is particularly enjoyed in British comedy, so we should consider the use of verbal comedy and the forms it may take.

Verbal humour in programmes like *Blackadder* mainly focuses on the sarcastic personality of the main character and the audience enjoy it more because we laugh along with Blackadder and mock the other characters' stupidity (in the second, third and fourth series that is – Blackadder himself was much more of a ridiculous figure in the first series). This is generally the premise of verbal wit: it relies on intelligence and quickness in response to other people's mistakes. Comic timing is an important aspect of both verbal and visual comedy, even though the pleasure in the outcome of these two comic forms is so different.

Wit and sarcasm don't always have to be in response to someone else's behaviour in a direct sense and certainly isn't always called for – but it is still funny as it is this unreasonable quality of the characters from which we gain pleasure. Wit and sarcasm are terms similar to humour and comedy, in that they are so closely related they are almost interchangeable and the difference between them seems to be all about intention. The general dictionary definition is that 'wit is the clever use of ideas or language intended to cause humorous affects in writing or speech', where as sarcasm is the same sort of thing but the intention is to insult another person. Therefore to be witty is regarded a good thing but to be defined as sarcastic is not.

So other characters around the protagonist, who have to suffer their unnecessary rages, have a vital role to play in the pleasure audiences gain from wit and sarcasm. This is rarely the wives of central male characters such as Victor Meldrew or Basil Fawlty as they are either feared or respected. In *One Foot in the Grave*, Victor's long-suffering wife is generally calm and unperturbed by his behaviour and even Sybil in *Fawlty Towers* rarely reacts to her husband's loss of temper. It is these responses that infuriate the men even more and cause yet more pleasure for audiences.

Verbal wit can also lead to other comic strategies being utilised. For example, Rik's sarcastic remarks in *The Young Ones* would generally lead to him getting hit by Vivien and therefore this led to physical humour being used, generally in the form of slapstick.

Playing around with words can also be an important element of verbal humour. Using words incorrectly like Del in *Only Fools and Horses* causes audiences to laugh at him rather than with him. This might seem cruel in normal circumstances but regular audiences are well aware of Del's pretensions so this is why it is legitimate to laugh at him. Characters who don't use English 'properly' have often been the butt of British humour, such as Manuel in *Fawlty Towers* or most of the cast in *Mind Your Language*. This is now generally seen as inappropriate, though strong regional and 'Received Pronunciation' accents are still often an important aspect of modern situation comedy.

Another common facet of British humour is the deliberate play on words to create a possible risqué comment, such as Mrs Slocombe always referring to her 'pussy' in *Are You Being Served?* (1972–1985). This kind of slightly cheeky wordplay was particularly popular in the 60s and 70s.

Thus, verbal humour plays a large part in the pleasure for the audience in situation comedy. Certain sitcoms will favour a particular style of verbal humour and it is important to consider which methods are being used in the sitcoms you study. This will tell you about intended audiences and intended pleasures for those audiences. An intellectually sarcastic main character, played by someone like Stephen Fry, will not appear in a comedy like *Two Pints of Lager (and a Packet of Crisps)* (2001–) because the intended audience is a younger one. This remark is not intended to insult this audience, it is merely referring to audience expectations and this links to scheduling, performance and intention. The same character would not appear in *The Royle Family*, but this is not to say this isn't a very cleverly constructed programme. It is simply that we have expectations of an actor like Fry that would not fit in with these programmes.

Physical humour, mainly slapstick, is still popular in many comedy shows although it is often derided as a simplistic comedy form. Comic timing and clever manipulation of an actor's physicality are nonetheless characteristics of physical humour. Using physical humour is a highly developed skill and actors become well known for their prowess in this area. It often works well in sketch shows because it is linked to ridiculous and unlikely situations. Also, the physical realisation of humour can be quite instant which also suits the sketch show format more than sitcom. In situation comedy, physical humour can be something that is built up to throughout an episode, the climax to a particular plot line; for example, the classic episode of *Only Fools and Horses* ('A Touch of Glass') where a priceless chandelier drops to the floor because Del and Rodney are waiting underneath the wrong one to catch it.

Other sitcoms, such as *Bottom* or *Father Ted* can use exaggerated physical humour all the way through, such as characters throwing themselves through windows. Because these programmes are not meant to be realistic, audiences accept the violence and physical mayhem often imperative to the storyline. Audiences are made aware of the lack of realism from other factors such as the characters, the set and the storylines; they may be slightly linked to likely events and situations and are often highly exaggerated or extreme. We therefore accept when someone gets hit in the face with a frying pan that it is 'cartoon' humour and the character involved will survive for the next episode.

Programmes like *Bottom* and *The Young Ones* enjoyed the same kind of comedy violence of the vaudeville performers, mainly because of the performances of Rik Mayall and Ade Edmondson who openly admire the form. Again, comedy performance is an important aspect of physical humour and slapstick, a form many comedy actors are famous for using in film and television.

Other important comic strategies include comic surprise and comic suspense. These terms can refer to action within the programme or to the position of the audience. So basically the audience or characters can be surprised or kept in suspense. Comic surprise is when something suddenly happens that we or the characters are not expecting and the consequences of this are funny. Comic surprise can relate to unexpected events, or characters behaving unexpectedly. This is not often a complete surprise to audiences as we are usually informed of more elements of the narrative than the characters involved, so the surprise is usually for the characters. We gain our pleasure from their misunderstanding or confusion caused by what happens.

There are two main methods of implementing a suspense plot in a situation comedy. One method is through the scheming and plotting of one or more characters so the suspense revolves around whether they will get away with it or not and if the characters they are trying to fool will find them out.

The other method of creating suspense is the opposite of this, where characters' misunderstanding of events and situations leads to suspense. These are the kinds of plots where characters get things wrong either through their lack of worldly knowledge, their arrogance or possibly their stupidity. In Basil Fawlty's case it is usually all three!

Case Study: *Fawlty Towers*

'The Wedding Party'
episode of *Fawlty Towers*

John Cleese brought a lot of his *Monty Python*-esque style to this short-running situation comedy. This is mainly therefore physical, slapstick humour. Written by himself and his then partner Connie Booth, who played Polly the waitress, the comedy in *Fawlty Towers* centred on Basil Fawlty's over the top reaction to practically everything. Basil had a strong sense of his social superiority, which was often a source of the comedy. He sees his small mindedness as a sign of his higher social values, but other characters often laugh at him or think he's completely mad.

For example, in Series 1, Episode 3 ('The Wedding Party'), a young unmarried couple have booked a room and are keen to ensure they have a double bed in their room. Basil, of course, does not approve, as he has certain values relating to sex before marriage, which he no doubt feels makes him superior. The comedy escalates based around Basil's exaggerated fears that all sorts of terrible extra-marital behaviour is going on his hotel. He runs around with a manic look on his face and his long legs leaping up and down stairs, creating physical humour just by his general demeanour. John Cleese's physicality is a large part of the audience's pleasure in this comedy and is used in many other episodes to create humour.

The parents of the young woman arrive as they are all going to a wedding, and they also know Polly. The humour occurs when Basil opens the door to the parent's room and first of all sees the man hugging the scantily clad young woman – who unbeknown to Basil is his daughter. This typical humour of misunderstanding continues throughout – where the audience are privy to more information than the central character. The regular use of comic suspense is an important element in *Fawlty Towers*. Our amusement as an audience is often due to Basil's lack of knowledge surrounding a particular event or character.

Basil, of course, assumes everyone is having sex with everyone else, because he is himself totally inept socially and sexually. However, the other interesting aspect to this episode is the glamorous French antique dealer that keeps flirting with Basil. He loves the attention but does not know how to deal with it; and placed alongside all the other behaviour that Basil thinks is going on, it makes this episode even funnier. All the misunderstandings could easily be resolved if Basil were less uptight.

Basil's over the top reaction to everything means he seems to be constantly on the verge of a nervous breakdown. He shouts, throws himself on the floor and is involved in lots of slapstick violence involving the ever-suffering waiter from Barcelona, Manuel, is where most of the physical humour is featured. Manuel might be hit in the head with a frying pan, a typical slapstick instrument of violence, and often the height difference between him and Basil can cause amusement as Basil looms over him or throws him over his shoulder to take him out of the way. Basil's violent reactions create opportunities for slapstick and his rude comments to his guests often involve deliberate misunderstandings or sarcasm.

Surreal comedy and the mainstream

Situation comedy does not have to be realistic, so writers have a lot of freedom when creating comedy. Some situation comedies are quite surreal and here writers can create bizarre characters and ridiculous situations that will still make people laugh, often because the situation is so silly. Situation comedies like *Father Ted* and *The IT Crowd* have surreal elements but they still give us a familiar setting, e.g. the workplace, or figures in the community we can recognise, e.g. priests.

Slapstick can often play an important role in surrealism, as physical humour like this can break the boundaries set by more realistic forms. This breaking of the audience's suspension of disbelief is relatively common in comedy and particularly suits those with a surreal edge.

The Young Ones is a good example as its rebellious, punk style gave a lot of scope to develop bizarre plots. One such storyline revolved around the attack of Neil's killer sock! In this episode the student's lack of laundering had led to Neil's sock being so dirty it came alive and terrorised the household. Inanimate objects and rats spoke directly to camera quite regularly in The Young Ones as did the leading characters.

A more modern surreal comedy is The Mighty Boosh, which centres on the adventures of two very different characters that are friends. Each episode contains a strange character and/or setting and involves a situation that is so outrageously ridiculous and fantastical, that audiences find them hilarious. Aimed at a teenage-to-mid 20s audience, The Mighty Boosh is the British comedy of the moment. It stars Julian Barrett and Noel Fielding and it began on BBC3 May 2004, though before this it was a live stage show and radio programme.

Barrett and Fielding play the central characters Howard Moon and Vince Noir, and are a typical sitcom duo in that they don't generally get on and have quite different personalities. It is definitely not your typical sitcom in the way it uses bizarre characters and interludes where the moon talks, but it does have a short series structure made up of episodes that last half an hour. Each episode has a stand alone narrative as each week a new bizarre scenario unfolds.

The Mighty Boosh could be compared to The Young Ones, as they both challenge situation comedy conventions of their day. The Mighty Boosh is a visual feast with dream-like situations and character. There is little sense of realism, reminiscent of Vic Reeves Big Night Out (1990–91). Musical interludes also play a part in the show, a vaudevillian technique also used by The Young Ones.

In the first series the two main characters work in a zoo but in the second they live in a flat with Naboo, a Shamen and talking gorilla Bollo, who were also in the first series. Vince is totally obsessed with his appearance and looks like a glam rock star from the 70s where as Howard strives to be recognised for his intellectual prowess. The whole programme has a 70s feel to it due to the costume, psychedelic music and visuals. The studio sets and costumes resemble a school production, which add to the humour of the series.

The series is set to become a cult comedy like *The Young Ones* and *Red Dwarf*, and for similar reasons. It appeals to a young audience, it challenges expectations of the situation comedy genre and it is has an anarchic edge. The weirdness of *The Mighty Boosh* and its witty main characters isolates older audiences with more traditional tastes in sitcom making it even more appealing to educated, young audiences.

Considering why these kinds of comedies are popular, and who with, could make an interesting discussion in your classes. You and your students may share some tastes and not others when it comes to sitcoms and humour in general. Younger people tend to enjoy things they think are a bit different from the norm be it fashion, music or comedy; and *The Mighty Boosh* certainly comes under this category just as *The Young Ones* did in an earlier era.

Performance style

When analysing an actor's performance in a film or drama, we generally refer to the 'quality' of their acting, but in comedy we also tend to consider other aspects of the actor's performance. This is because we see the role of the comedy actor as different to that of other actors. They do not merely play a part as directed or defined by the writer; they bring their skills as a comedian or comedy actor to the role. That is why comedy actors and writers often work together on various projects, or why many comedians write parts for themselves. In some sitcoms, the comedians manage to incorporate their actual stand up routines into the programme, as the premise of the show involves this job, as in *Seinfeld* and *Home Improvement* (1991–99).

Costume and physical appearance along with the use of voice and physical expression are all important tools of the comedy actor and these elements are skilfully implemented to create appropriate humour in various sitcoms. The importance of one of these aspects over another depends very much on the style of the comedy. Costume is an important aspect of any show as it establishes character, time and setting. But in *Absolutely Fabulous* the costumes of Eddie, Patsy, Bubbles and Saffie were an important part of the humour. Eddie and Patsy always had to wear the latest fashion labels and Saffie was the complete antithesis of this wearing twee cardigans and prudish skirts. Bubbles' style was more unique, mocking the clothes of the 'über cool'. The characters worked in the shallow world of fashion and the costume choices knowingly commented on this world and its fickleness.

Well known characters in situation comedies often have distinctive voices, mannerisms or turns of phrase. Sometimes they have a certain phrase that they repeat throughout the episodes. This gives audiences something they can anticipate hearing from their favourite character in each episode. Accents are important, and often part of the pleasure of a comedy is the accents and use of colloquialisms, such as Father Jack's 'feck' in *Father Ted* and Del Boy's 'lovely jubbly'. Some may consider it patronising to laugh at accents but it is an enjoyment in the use of language that amuses us rather than laughing directly at an accent.

For some comic actors their physical expression is key to their performance, body language, facial expressions and physical movement being all part of their repertoire. Michael Crawford brought a lot of his skills as a performer to the character of Frank Spencer in *Some Mothers Do 'Ave 'Em*. He created a quiet, child-like voice, innocent facial expression and a stance that showed a character seemingly unaware of what to do with his arms in normal situations. Frank Spencer was naïve and totally inept, always landing in ridiculous situations that created considerable mayhem.

4. Comic Structure

As outlined in the Introduction to this *Guide*, there are three basic structures that situation comedy narratives are based around: where one main character is at the centre of the narrative; a scenario based around a partnership, and a story focusing on a group of characters. At first glance it may seem pretty obvious that situation comedies are going to be based around one of these three structures, as any programme looking at human relationships has to look at a group, a partnership or an individual. The reason why it is interesting to consider these structures (in any narrative, really) is because of the way the structures affect other aspects of the programme; and also because within them there are other typical formats that tend to be adhered to.

The reason I mention other narratives is because other television genres also use these structures, particularly narratives centred on partnerships. The most common television drama set around partnerships is police dramas; but ensemble casts are also common in other workplace shows such as hospital dramas. In fact crime dramas use all three possible structures that situation comedies adhere to – team, partners and individual – because of the different roles within law enforcement (which may make an interesting comparison to situation comedies but it's not something to dwell on here).

This comparison to other genres is relevant because situation comedies can be set in the workplace; so workplace dramas are likely to share similarities with work-based sitcoms. Dramas set in the workplace focus on relationships between colleagues such as sexual affairs, and conflict between workers and their bosses. This may not sound the stuff of comedy but clashes between work colleagues happen in both genres, and affairs can be the source of humour in situation comedies.

For example, in *The Office* a huge 'will they won't they?' plot line developed around Dawn the receptionist and Tim, the nice, normal office worker. They flirt a lot at work and the viewers are invited to dislike her fiancé and hope she gets together with Tim. Of course, there are lots of near misses and torture for any romantically inclined viewers when Dawn leaves Wernham Hogg to move to

Florida. The Christmas 2003 special, though, brought them together at last in a satisfyingly, dramatic scene you would expect from drama rather than comedy. This use of devices so close to drama could be assigned to the fact that *The Office* is a parody of a documentary so in some ways it is likely to be more 'realistic'. But basically, a workplace comedy still has to offer audiences familiar situations, characters and events that they can relate to, as this is what makes the comedy work.

However, comedies such as *Fawlty Towers* or *Red Dwarf* could also be described as workplace sitcoms as the first of these is set in a hotel and the second on a working spaceship. Granted, not many of us can relate to the job of working on a space ship but there are engineers and cleaners who work in more ordinary places and do the same sort of job as Rimmer and Dave. There are also lots of people who work with ambitious and arrogant colleagues who think they deserve to be promoted, or work with bosses who over-react to problems and think they are better than anyone else.

So this is how writers of situation comedies involve audiences in workplace settings in the same way as dramas do. The situations, the characters, the settings are familia, but then they are twisted and exaggerated to the point where they are funny but grounded in 'reality'.

Structure 1 – The individual

There are many situation comedies focusing on one main character and these programmes tend to have numerous elements in common that you can discuss and analyse with students. The important thing to remember, though, when you start these discussions is that you are likely to spend some time arguing as to whether a programme is set around one character or whether other members of the cast are equally important. Indeed in some cases, situation comedies have started out with one structure and then other characters have developed so the format has changed to a partnership or an ensemble structure. It is a similar problem to that of looking at genre as a concept, but it is also a positive thing. We wouldn't want styles and structures to be entirely predictable and unchanging as this would make our experience of film and television rather boring. Also, engaging students in debate about such things makes them more aware of the complexities of genre and media concepts.

A situation comedy with one character that the narrative revolves around has to have a strong actor as the central figure. Generally these actors are well known in the realm of comedy or acting before taking on the role. Lots of comedians who began in the difficult area of stand up have moved into the more stable area of situation comedy as they have matured and they may take traits of their stand up routines or characters with them. Rik Mayall and Ade Edmondson developed the characters of Vivien and Rik on stage before *The Young Ones* and Nigel Planer also started off at The Comedy Club with a hippy character as part of his routine. Alan Partridge was a character who started off on radio for Steve Coogan.

Patricia Routledge, Richard Wilson and Warren Mitchell had careers as serious actors before moving into popular situation comedies. Other actors, like David Jason, were relatively unknown before catapulting to comedy fame. The thing that ties all these different performers together is their skill in comedy performance. We could never imagine anyone but Warren Mitchell playing Alf Garnett or Phil Silvers as Bilko – they *are* those characters to audiences.

Many of these central characters have personality traits in common too. They are almost tragi-comedy figures as they want to escape the situation they are in but there are always obstacles in their path to prevent this from happening. However, often these characters are quite dislikeable, so this is one of the reasons they don't achieve their goals; they don't deserve to. They are not as talented, intelligent or popular as they think they are. A lot of the humour then develops around their sense of reality, as opposed to our perception.

In other sitcoms, where the narrative mainly revolves around one main character but other characters play an imperative role in the narrative, these others are often largely responsible for preventing the main character from achieving their goals. They may go out of the way to spoil opportunities for fear of being left alone, as in *Steptoe and Son* (1962–74), or the main character may feel responsible for them or tied to the situation, as in *Father Ted*.

Some characters just know they are on to a good thing staying where they are, like Blackadder. Everyone else around him is stupid so he might as well feel superior to them all and get what he can out of them; while other individuals are trapped by circumstances like, Ronnie Barker's Fletcher in *Porridge*. He is likeable and witty but he is in prison so cannot escape his situation. Thus, many situation comedies, especially those focusing on an individual, are implicitly about being trapped. Trapped by circumstances, trapped by others or trapped through their own inadequacies.

Case Study: *Marion and Geoff*

I choose to focus on this comedy here because it does not fit neatly into the sitcom genre on initial viewing and the title may lead you to believe it is a partnership based comedy rather than one focused on an individual. *Marion and Geoff* (2000–03), though, is a series based around the monologues of Keith Barratt, who speaks directly to the audience through a camera mounted on the dashboard of his taxi cab and, in later series, the car he drives as a chauffeur. Marion is his ex-wife who has left him, taken his children and moved in with Geoff. In terms of style then, this is an interesting programme as the static camera and the setting present audiences with a documentary style piece that became popular in comedy in the early 2000s.

The other element to consider in this programme is performance. Rob Brydon is brilliant as the naïve Keith. Though he is the only character we see, he is no ranting Victor Meldrew or complaining Blackadder. Keith is lonely and abused but he always looks on the bright side. He makes excuses for his ex-wive's terrible behaviour and his life just gets worse and worse as the series progresses. It is his naïveté we laugh at. Audiences are meant to feel sorry for Keith but we can't help laughing at him. The camera acts as Keith's video diary, so is constantly set at a close-up angle to Keith as he talks to the camera mounted on his dashboard. This provides an intimacy to the narrative and a discomforting edge to our laughter, common in contemporary sitcoms.

The first series consisted of ten minute monologues so wasn't really a sitcom in the traditional sense; but the second series conformed to a six episode, thirty minute programme format which seems to fit the sitcom genre more neatly.

Structure 2 – Partnerships and groups

This 'trapped' narrative is common to other styles of situation comedies too. If there is conflict between characters, which is often at the heart of the comedy, then why else would characters stay together unless they felt trapped in some way? In *Red Dwarf*, for example, the characters are trapped together in space and you know that is the only reason Dave and Rimmer would ever talk to each other. A common reason partner based comedy characters stay together is because they are related, as in *Birds of a Feather* (1989–98) and *Steptoe and Son*. Conflict is a large part of comedy and in sitcoms characters need reasons to clash and they need reasons to stay together even if they do argue all the time.

Being related may not be enough, though, and in these two

programmes the characters in some way need the other one. In *Birds of a Feather* the two women lived together because their husbands were in prison so they needed the other's moral (and, in Sharon's case, financial) support.

Case Study: A Comparison of *Men Behaving Badly* and *Absolutely Fabulous*

Absolutey Fabulous

I would argue that both of these are examples of partnership sitcoms, even though other characters have a regular and often quite interesting part to play in plot development over the various series, it is the relationship between the two central characters, their interaction with others and situations that are the key to all storyline development.

Both sitcoms show two characters that no one else understands or appreciates – which is why the respective pairs are such close friends. Unlike a lot of this type of sitcom the two central characters share some very similar character traits and they are best friends. One is a bit more reliant on the other, but generally it is those two 'against the world'.

Men Behaving Badly (1992–98) and *Absolutely Fabulous* were both very popular in the 1990s and they make an interesting comparison because they were so similar yet very different in terms of style. Both shows represent drunk, outrageous, wild main characters but one represents young men and the other wealthy middle-aged women. Both sets of characters refuse to grow up and revel in their 'politically incorrect' views. The only value systems that seem to be respected are those of friendship. Self-respect, family values and respect for the older generation are all joyfully thrown aside!

The main difference in the two programmes is the social context. *Ab Fab's* Eddie and Patsy represent a higher social class than Gary and Tony in *Men Behaving Badly* and these differences helped make both shows successful. I don't think it would have worked the other way round – if the women sat at home drinking lager and the boys went out getting drunk on champagne! *Ab Fab* is probably one of the first sitcoms to show women who are 'old enough to know better', from middle class wealthy backgrounds, behaving outrageously.

But *Ab Fab* appealed to women who would love to be able to behave like Patsy every now and again. A lot of the jokes in the programme were also directed specifically at women, but the bad behaviour and slapstick that we would expect more from male-focused comedy, like *Men Behaving Badly*, appealed to both genders.

Men Behaving Badly

Preferred readings of *Men Behaving Badly* also meant it appealed to men and women. For men it celebrated the 'laddish' culture that became prevalent in the 90s. Gary and Tony celebrated this lad culture. However, women liked *Men Behaving Badly* because the witty, clever characters in this programme were the women. Gary's long suffering girlfriend Dorothy was superior to him in intelligence and wit; and Deborah toyed with Tony's affections for about two series. He always wanted her, more than the other way round, even when she gave in and actually started dating him.

Both of these programmes used physical humour, in the form of slapstick; *Ab Fab* also verged on the absurd at times and both used a lot of verbal wit and sarcasm. *Absolutely Fabulous* is very bright and colourful, portraying well the outlandish fashion ideas of the ultra trendy, whereas *Men Behaving Badly*'s setting reflected the lives of the two men, who are actually very conventional, aside from their (usually drunken) antics.

For characters to clash, then, they need a reason. A disruption to their regular lives is often the catalyst for the conflict between characters but their differing reactions to these circumstances is important too. Characters often have quite opposing personality traits in partnership or ensemble-based situation comedies. This may not be realistic but it doesn't have to be. Sitcoms, like soaps, miniaturise our experiences so that we can compare what is happening to various aspects and experiences in our own lives. Probably the most realistic clashes occur in family-based sitcoms and those set in the workplace. It doesn't matter how close we are to family members or how similar we are in genetic make-up, the fact that we all live in such close proximity to our family means clashes are common place, so audiences have a clear point of comparison. In the workplace we again have to sit side by side with people every day, but we cannot choose who they are, so conflicts are highly possible.

Structure 3 – Ensemble based sitcoms

In opposition to comedy programmes with one strong central character who stands out from the rest, so those with an ensemble cast have to develop a series of characters where no one person overshadows the others. This is not that difficult and in some ways gives comedy programmes more flexibility as they can develop multiple narratives and continuous sub-plots throughout each series. A perfect example of this would be *Friends*, as the changing relationships and experiences of the group of characters allowed for a very long running programme.

The other aspect a writer has to consider with an ensemble comedy is how to differentiate the characters from each other. There shouldn't be competition between the characters for narrative time but there has to be variety in the personality traits. In family-based sitcoms, then, there are often stereotypical differences between siblings. For example in *8 Simple Rules...for Dating My Teenage Daughter* (2002–05), a modern American sitcom shown on ABC, we have two teenage sisters. One is the pretty, blonde popular girl and the other is the intelligent, principled sister. Other representations in this programme are the mother, who is the one holding the family together, the younger brother, who is typically hormonal and mischievous, and the grandfather and the nephew (of the mother). These also add conflict to the family as they clash a lot.

The grandfather represents the grumpy old man, and the nephew is relaxed and immature with little direction in his life. The grandfather and the nephew are quite interesting representations and challenge the otherwise simplistic portrayal of family life, as the extended family is observed. Also, the grandfather is humorously lucid and does not fit the sugary, or indeed senile representation we often see of older people, particularly in comedy. The nephew is the most immature member of the family, who relies on his aunt for financial and moral support in many episodes. The humour presented here is the fact that he is in his late 30s and lives in his aunt's basement. (John Ritter played the father of the family in the first year of production, but when he died ABC decided to continue the series and his character also died.)

The element that is typical of family-based sitcoms, particularly American ones, is the moral aspect, the message of each episode usually involving the importance of family values. Whatever conflict has occurred in each show, we usually see the family rallying together in the end and clarifying the strength of their relationship.

So, in this programme, and many other family-based sitcoms like it, we have a microcosm of American family life. It doesn't represent a realistic family – except for the arguing – because often people related to each other are similar. In sitcoms, families often have huge personality differences and intellectual capabilities which seems unlikely for characters that share genetic make-up and the same upbringing. We accept this as an audience in the same way as we accept how so many horrible things can happen in one street in a soap opera: soaps and sometimes sitcoms represent elements of many people's experiences squashed into one place.

In workplace-based situation comedies it is easier to construct characters with differences because there can be characters from various social backgrounds and domestic situations working in the same place. People have different views of their career, with some taking it more seriously than others; and friendships, gossiping, arguments and affairs do happen in real workplaces, providing the comedy writer with stacks of material.

Scrubs is an American hospital-based sitcom, first aired in 2001. It follows the lives of three young residents (JD, Turk and Elliot) embarking on their medical careers at Sacred Heart Hospital. Though filmed in a real hospital, with some storylines based around the difficulties of the medical profession, the dream sequences and special effects used add a certain surreal quality, not normally associated with realism. The use of static shots with the set appearing to move brings audiences closer to the action. We see everything through JD's eyes, so along with his narrative voiceover we are also privy to his fantasy sequences, giving us further insight into his fears and dreams.

The plots mainly focus on the relationships and personal difficulties of the central characters, so moments of comedy can often be punctuated by moving performances. Combining witty dialogue, detailed characterisation and interesting filming techniques, *Scrubs* has many features appropriate for textual analysis.

5. Audiences and Institutions

TV channels and sitcoms

It is ITV that the UK has to thank for the situation comedy. Before commercial television (1955) there were very few sitcoms. Any comedy programmes were, until this point, imported from the US where the cable television network system was more commercial than the BBC, whose emphasis was on educating audiences rather than amusing them. It was only when the BBC monopoly was eliminated and they had competition that they began producing a greater variety of light entertainment.

Comedy is a risky business and some programmes can be expensive to produce so broadcasters do not want to get it wrong when they are commissioning new programmes. Lots of shows that end up on terrestrial channels started their life with smaller audiences, on radio or digital channels, or originated in other countries. Comedy programmes are often produced in-house by the BBC but are bought in from independent sources or imported from TV channels abroad on other channels. For the UK, most situation comedy imports are from the US. Although Australia also provides the UK with a lot of programmes, these are not often sitcoms, though *Kath and Kim* proved popular with some of the British audience.

Comedy is important to broadcasters as it is one of the most popular of TV genres. Traditional, studio-based sitcoms are cheap to produce as they use reoccurring sets and a regular cast; however, recent years have seen a rise in sketch shows, comedy-based quizzes and comedy drama, and a decline in situation comedy. Channels usually have dedicated departments to deal with their comedy programming and new comedy has been an important factor in the development of digital channels, especially BBC3. BBC3 specialises in new comedy programmes and drama. Here is where such programmes as *Little Britain* (2003–06) and *The Catherine Tate Show* (2004–) started before moving over to a more mainstream channel as they proved to be a hit with a wider audience.

The introduction of digital Freeview channels has meant more comedy than ever before is available to UK audiences. The ABC channel has US comedy hits such as *Hope & Faith* (2003–06) and *8 Simple Rules* in regular slots each evening. Repeats of old classic sitcoms such as *Rising Damp* (1974–78) can also be viewed on ITV3. The types of comedy programme channels choose to commission can be an important way they identify themselves to target audiences. BBC3, as already mentioned, is where the BBC can be more experimental with their comedy programming. If programmes are successful there, they may then move to a more mainstream spot on BBC2.

Channel 4's first transmissions coincided with alternative comedy's transition from stage to television. Where the BBC was more cautious, Channel 4's remit was to offer programmes with a more controversial edge, so alternative comedy was just the thing. Since its commencement in 1982, Channel 4 has been committed to producing comedy for less mainstream audiences. This began with *The Comic Strip Presents...* (1982–), and developed into programmes like *Desmond's* (1989–94) produced in conjunction with the Black Theatre Co-operative, where the whole team of actors, writers and producers came from the black community.

Channel 4 have also taken on comedians and comedy programmes that other channels rejected as too extreme, although now, BBC3 seems to be allowing the BBC more freedom to experiment with less mainstream comedians and styles. As well as succeeding with their own comedy productions, Channel 4 have secured some very popular US imports, probably the most significant being *Friends*. Prior to this C4 acquired the very popular *Cheers* and *Roseanne*, then *Frasier* (1993–2004) (a spin off from *Cheers*) and more recently *Will & Grace* (1998–2006).

According to the BBC's website (July 2007), their priority at the moment is to commission traditional, studio-based sitcoms that can reach a mainstream audience on BBC1. For BBC2 they want more diverse comedy particularly from black and Asian writers. Channel 4, however, whose initial aim was to be innovative and exciting, seems to be happy to move away from sitcom. In a briefing session of their Entertainment & Comedy department, documented on the Channel 4 website (July 07), comments were made regarding how panel-based comedy quiz shows were a good place to test comedy talent; and that they were looking for a new idea for yet another reality show. They are however producing six one-off sitcoms for C4's twenty-fifth anniversary (November 2007), with the possibility that they could be made into series.

Production

The production cycle of a sitcom starts with the commissioning of the script. Channels usually have departments dedicated to the commissioning of comedy programmes; and scripts and ideas can be received in a variety of ways. Though Channel 4 will only accept work through agents and production companies, both Channel 4 and the BBC have departments specifically designed to nurture new talent.

It can take up to 20 weeks for a proposal to be considered. Some writers send in scripts through comedy actors they know or have worked with before and if the writer is also known the production process has a slight head start. However, there will still be casting, set construction and rehearsals in the pre-production of any programme before the production can begin.

Depending on the complexity and the style of the sitcom, the production process can be very different. Traditional sitcoms filmed before a studio audience with a three camera set-up will be quite cheap to produce as they use a limited amount of sets and standard production values. If a comedy uses outdoor filming and a more cinematic style in general, with on-location shooting and high production values, it will be more expensive to shoot and take longer to produce. Programmes like *Ugly Betty* (2006–) will have a much bigger budget than *8 Simple Rules*, but it is evident when watching these two US programmes that they are constructed very differently.

Post-production starts with editing, and, again, sitcoms without studio audiences will have more footage to edit, but the promotion of the programme will depend on the target audience and the channel involved.

When marketing a new programme there are various techniques used. By advertising the new programme immediately before or after an established comedy, a large potential audience can be reached. If a new comedy programme is targeting a certain age range, for example, the youth market, it may advertise next to a different genre of programme that is targeted at that age. Channel 4 and E4, for example, advertise each other's programmes as the channels are used in different ways by audiences, and E4 is particularly popular with the teen market.

Writers and producers

Another interesting aspect to contemplate when looking at the production of comedy programmes and situation comedy is looking at the writers, actors and producers responsible for various works. In American and British comedy we see the same names crop up time and time again and if you become familiar with the genre, it is not difficult to identify the work of particular writers and even production companies.

Baby Cow Productions, for example, is the company established by the well known comedy writers/actors, Steve Coogan and Henry Normal. They have been very successful with programmes such as *The Mighty Boosh*, *Nighty Night* (2004–05) and *Marion and Geoff*. Their website describes their favoured comedy programming as 'cutting edge', 'bold and innovative' and certainly they seem to favour comedy that is darker or more abstract.

Hat Trick Productions are another highly successful company having produced the situation comedies *Drop the Dead Donkey* (1990–98) and *Father Ted* as well as other comedy programmes such as *The Kumars at No. 42* (2001–), *Have I Got News for You* (1990–) and *Room 101* (1994–).

Comedy programming is unusual in that the writers are almost as well known as comedy actors. In Britain, in particular, the relationship between actors and writers seems to be a crucial part of their mutual success; and writers and actors will work together time and time again on different comedy projects. Indeed, the role of actor and writer are often merged, with many actors being involved in writing shows they star in, such as Ronnie Barker, Rowan Atkinson, Jennifer Saunders and Steve Coogan. Ricky Gervais and Stephen Merchant wrote, directed and starred in the popular series *Extras*, an interesting programme to mention in a chapter on institutions, seeing as it is largely about the media.

In Britain, comedy writers tend to work in partnership or individually and there are various writers that over the years have gained recognition for their style of writing. This is true of the work of David Croft, for example, a well established writer who has been producing comedy for over 30 years. Croft's work has a clearly identifiable style that has been popular with large audiences throughout his career. His jokes are traditional, the issues he looks at are light-hearted and the comedy actors he uses are known for their conventional comedy range.

Croft wrote well known comedies such as *It Ain't Half Hot Mum* (with Jimmy Perry), *Are You Being Served?* (with Jeremy Lloyd) and *'Allo 'Allo!* (1982–1992, again with Lloyd). Croft also constructed a series of comedy shows that used the same set of actors. Although the characters they played were quite similar in these programmes, they were set in different historical times and places. Using an ensemble cast, it's not surprising these programmes were set in some type of workplace. *Hi-De-Hi!* (with Perry) was the first, then *You Rang, M'Lord?* (1988–1993, again with Perry) and then *Oh, Doctor Beeching!* (1995–1997, with Richard Spendlove).

Most of Croft's popular sitcoms were reminiscent of a different era and looked at these times with a gentle humour. What is interesting about Croft's work, though, is the pre-occupation with social class. In *Dad's Army* (1968–1977, with Jimmy Perry), for example, Capt. Mainwaring's civilian job is that of a bank manager. He is middle management and as far as he is concerned has earned his respect. He has no time for Sgt. Wilson, who may be of higher social standing than him but is of lower rank. This does not bother Wilson; he doesn't seem to care about respect and takes the procedures and petty bureaucracy of the Home Guard much less seriously than Mainwaring. Consequently, his relaxed and laid back attitude constantly infuriates the Captain.

Social class is also an important aspect of *Hi-De-Hi!*. Ted, the brash working class comedian, has no respect for the university educated manager of the holiday camp, Mr Fairbrother. Clashes between them, which generally involve Ted getting one up on his boss, are one of the common plot lines in many episodes. *You Rang, M'Lord?* revolved around social class in a sense, as it followed the antics of a household of servants in an upper class stately home.

Dick Clement and Ian La Frenais are a famous comedy writing partnership that focused more on ordinary, working class men and were keen on realism, both in the situations they represented and the dialogue they wrote. They wrote *The Likely Lads* (1964–66), *Porridge* (1974–77) and *Auf Wiedersehen, Pet* (1983–1986), their work also spanning over more than 30 years, yet maintaining a perceptive observance of the humour and warmth in the life of the working class man.

Richard Curtis, the most recent of these 'brand name' comedy writers, makes an interesting contrast. Curtis was educated at Oxford and was involved with the alternative comedy scene in the 1980s, writing for *Spitting Image* and *Not the Nine O'Clock News* (1979–1982). He is now best known for his contribution to the British film industry and the representation of middle class Britain in films like *Notting Hill* (1999) and *Four Weddings and a Funeral* (1994). But prior to this Curtis made a significant contribution to the situation comedy genre.

It was at Oxford that Richard Curtis met Rowan Atkinson and they worked together on the *Blackadder* series and, later, the *Mr. Bean* TV show (1990–1995). Curtis's speciality is dry wit and, again, he is a writer who has worked with the same actors repeatedly, such as Rowan Atkinson and Hugh Grant, in his films. Curtis began his writing when comedy was highly political and there has definitely been a development, if not regression, in his style and the kind of work he has done – the starting point being *Not the Nine O'Clock News*, an anarchic, mock news programme starring Griff Rhys Jones and Mel Smith, and the last sitcom he produced being *The Vicar Of Dibley*. All of Curtis's work has proved highly popular with large audiences as he seems to capture a familiar, if not exactly 'realistic', aspect of 'Britishness' in his work.

Considering the work of individual writers is an interesting task and allows students to consider comic strategies, representation, and social and cultural contexts. The time in which a writer's work is being produced has to be an influence on their output in one way or another. In Curtis's case it was a direct influence on his early work, as he looked at topical issues. In the other featured writers, topical issues were raised through the characterisations they portrayed, with Croft emphasising the differences between social classes and Clement and La Frenias celebrating working class life.

New writers, new styles

Developing new programmes that capture ever-changing and more demanding audiences is a difficult job and comedy programmes in particular have to try and satisfy the censors as well as wide-ranging audiences with differing tastes. Ricky Gervais is one of the most well-known names in contemporary comedy. Starting his career in a radio station, where he gained his own show, Gervais went on to collaborate with Stephen Merchant to produce *The Office*, which was first aired on BBC2 in 2001.

The Office received massive critical acclaim and was hugely popular with audiences, with the DVD of the first series being Britain's biggest selling non-film title. The faux-documentary style of the sitcom was reflective of the new style, fly-on-the-wall reality shows taking television by storm (but in fact they had originally shot their demo in this way because it was easy and quick).

The Office spoke to a large proportion of British people, particularly those in their 20s and 30s stuck in similar office jobs; but it was the characters and subsequent performance of the actors in *The Office* that resonated. This style of comedy rarely used 'jokes'.

The use of fly-on-the-wall techniques brought audiences close to the action, resulting in sometimes uneasy but still humorous viewing. Close-ups and hand held cameras portrayed private interactions that within the diegetic world of the show were not meant for public eyes and as characters spoke directly to cameras we had further insight into their views and desires.

David Brent, the manager of the Wernham Hogg office, played by Gervais, was the central character. Everything about him made audiences cringe. He was politically incorrect, professionally inept, thought all his colleagues loved him when they, like us, knew he was an idiot. Brent was a totally unsympathetic character and offset against the documentary style this offered a rare viewing experience. A realistic style alongside such a ridiculous, arrogant character made for initially uncomfortable viewing. Evidently, considering its popularity, *The Office* was something viewers were ready for.

Extras, the eagerly awaited follow up to *The Office*, was aired on BBC2 in 2005. Gervais and Merchant had not rushed to create their next show and though *Extras* did not gain quite the same acclaim of *The Office*, it was still a popular and critical hit. Again, the central character was played by Ricky Gervais, but Andy Millman, the struggling writer and actor he played, was a much more likeable character than David Brent.

It was the comedy of mishaps and mistakes that attracted audiences to *Extras*. Though *Extras* didn't introduce a new style or structure to the sitcom form, what set it apart was the plethora of guest stars Gervais and Merchant managed to attract. The reputation they had established with *The Office* was essential to the success of this programme, as was making connections in the celebrity world. David Bowie, Kate Winslet and even Robert De Niro all starred in episodes of *Extras* and were happy to mock aspects of their star status or media image. The situations Andy and Maggie, his friend and fellow extra, found themselves in were funny, but the celebrity guest was the element that made this show special.

Thus, Merchant and Gervais mark a new development in sitcom writing. With *The Office* and *Extras*, they have not produced traditional, studio-based sitcoms with canned laughter and a three camera set-up, but whether they intentionally set out to turn situation comedy on its head is debatable. They merely came up with exciting ideas and characters and used the structure that best suited their narrative intentions. *The Office* could have been filmed in a studio in front of a live audience, but this would have significantly changed the way audiences experience the characters. Without the discomfort of the documentary style the viewing experience would have been entirely different.

Case Study: *Peep Show*

The first series of *Peep Show* was broadcast on Channel 4 in 2003 and, like *The Office*, it suggested a new direction for sitcoms. Starring the up and coming comedy duo, David Mitchell and Robert Webb, *Peep Show* indeed allowed audiences to see things they shouldn't see. Though the characters of Jeremy and Mark were pretty unlikeable, audiences were forced to view the narrative through their eyes, literally. All of the action is viewed through point of view shots from one of the main characters; sometimes this actually involved a camera strapped to the actor's head to truly portray their point of view. And to further involve the viewer, narrative voiceovers told us what horrible thoughts were running through their minds.

The programme had an uncomfortable intimacy, similar to *The Office* but achieved it in a very different way. Here, the characters are unaware of the audience's existence but in *The Office* the presence of the camera is part of the narrative. In *Peep Show*, the audience is literally in the characters' heads which is an unusual and uncomfortable place to be.

The writers of *Peep Show* are Sam Baine and Jesse Armstrong, who, after writing as part of a bigger team on children's sitcoms *Kerching!* (2003–06) and *My Parents Are Aliens* (1999–2006), have also written for the sketch shows *Smack the Pony* (1999–2003) and *Velvet Soup* (2001). They met on a creative writing course at Manchester

University and both worked in other areas before becoming a full-time writing team in 1997. The first series of *Peep Show* won the Rose d'Or for Best Comedy Show 2003.

Audience pleasures

The pleasures audiences receive from the experience of watching situation comedy are varied. The most basic reason audiences enjoy comedy is obvious – it makes us laugh. But there are other levels on which situation comedy works. Some of these have been mentioned in other chapters, as the details of how and why comedy works have a habit of connecting to each other.

First it is important to consider why audiences laugh. Generally in situation comedy we are either laughing at someone or with someone and our pleasure is often satisfied on both of these levels. Comedy often has a social aspect: we want to share our laughter with others, by sharing jokes and by watching situation comedies either with others or replaying our favourite parts to each other the next day. We are often invited to laugh at other characters, putting ourselves in a superior position to the characters in the programme – we would never behave in such an outrageous way or react like that. We are often further reassured that this is OK because of the addition of canned laughter, which also adds a social aspect if we are watching the comedy alone.

Socialisation is further enhanced by the inclusion of catchphrases that we can share with out friends. Though comic surprise may be an important part of humour, it is common for audiences to watch their favourite sitcoms time and time again. People practically learn the scripts off by heart so they can re-enact their favourite moments with friends, so making predictability a seemingly contradictory factor in comedy's success.

Audiences are usually placed in an omniscient position to the narrative as another pleasure is that of knowing more than the characters involved in the action. In fact, it is often a crucial aspect of the plot that audiences are subject to information characters don't know, and that is what makes the situation, their reaction or the outcome so funny.

However, some situation comedies have challenged these common aspects of the genre and presented us with new techniques and styles that don't use these reassuring methods. Some modern sitcoms do not use canned laughter and the new penchant for a documentary style of filming has led to audiences losing their superior position and having to gain their comedy pleasure in new ways. Programmes like *The Office* and *Marion and Geoff*, in particular, directly involve audiences; the characters speak directly to them using the camera as a way of communicating their feelings or personality traits they think others find endearing.

These kinds of programme work in the same way as such reality TV shows as *I'm a Celebrity, Get Me Out of Here!* (2002–) and *Big Brother* (1999–): they offer audiences voyeuristic insights into people's lives. In comedy this is fictional, but the premise is still the same. Audiences are often made to feel uncomfortable by a character's behaviour in these new fly-on-the-wall documentaries because we see ordinary people, and even celebrities, often unguarded and mentally unravelling because of the situations they are put in. *Peep Show*, as already mentioned, gives us added insight into the main characters psyche with the use of voiceover narratives. Through this we learn more about the characters than the people around them so we are given an uncomfortable sort of omniscient position – sometimes we do not *want* to know what another person is thinking.

So there are many levels at which comedies involve audiences, but as discussed previously in the *Guide*, finding something funny is an individual response, though we may want to share this experience to enhance it. Different people laugh at different things and sharing the humour of a situation is, in some ways, about fitting in. Young people, especially, will share their comedy pleasures with their peers and those that don't find a programme funny will, to a certain extent, not fit in to that social grouping.

Some situation comedy is very specifically targeted at a particular demographic and this is especially evident in comedy aimed at a youth audience. *The Young Ones*, as part of alternative comedy's attempt to turn situation comedy on its head and aim it at a different audience, was purposefully crude and anarchic. It intended to alienate older audiences and draw in a new, younger audience who rejected the middle class suburban style prevalent in sitcoms at the time. *Red Dwarf* also became a cult situation comedy: its setting in space attracted a young, sci-fi loving audience, but it was the repetition of crude phrases like 'smeg head' that mainly interested younger audiences.

Many situation comedies have a wider, family orientated audience in mind and some are targeting the older generation while still maintaining a wider appeal. Again performance is covered in other area of this *Guide*, but as well as being an important element in humour, star performance is an important element in considering audience appeal. Audiences are loyal to comedy performers in a similar way to how they may be loyal to film or pop stars. If we find a comedian that we have seen doing stand up funny, or have heard them on the radio, we are more inclined to watch them in a new situation comedy on television. Comedy actors, though they may play various roles in their comedy careers, will still have a certain appeal because of the style of the work they are known for. Steve Coogan, for example, may appeal to audiences who remember his Paul Calf days, even though his work has become more wide-ranging and sophisticated as his career has progressed.

Ronnie Barker has quite a wide appeal as a performer due to his ability to take on an interesting wide range of characters. This was evident in *The Two Ronnies*, the sketch show he performed with Ronnie Corbett but continued to be so in the sitcoms he was famous for – *Porridge, Open All Hours* (1976–1985) and *Clarence* (1988). Comedy performers have a similar 'star' appeal to film stars. If we like them in one programme we are likely to watch them in another, because audiences know what kind of humour appeals to them so the sitcom per se may not be as important as the comedy star who is in it.

Themes and issues

Situation comedies reflect things that are happening in society. That's not to say that they are directly about situations in the present, but that they reflect changes in attitudes in our society and different elements of culture. For example, *Friends* is about a group of young people who mainly stay single into their 30s. This reflects current changes in lifestyles. *Men Behaving Badly* represented a laddish culture that was prevalent in the 90s, while *Will & Grace* shows a gay man and straight woman sharing a house and the storylines reflect how society is more accepting of alternative lifestyles.

If you watch sitcoms from the 70s you may be shocked by some comments and themes in programmes such as *Mind Your Language* and *Love Thy Neighbour*. Today these would seem quite racist, while others would seem sexist or homophobic to modern audiences.

As previously noted many sitcoms are based around some sort of community, the workplace or the family. These settings are instantly recognisable to audiences. As in soap operas, audiences need to be able to compare themselves to characters, particularly their situations and relationships with others. It is the relationships that we associate with, the desire for friendship and support or of feeling trapped and wanting to escape a situation.

Social class is an important aspect in many situation comedies in Britain, perhaps because it is such an important part of our history. In Britain it has had a major influence on our development as a country and so has influenced Britain's writers of drama, comedy and theatre. There are a range of situation comedies by writers that focus on working class attitudes and beliefs, the clashes between social classes and the comedy caused because of these different attitudes. But social class is not the only issue important to Britain's comedy writers and as already suggested this theme is more relevant to social and historical factors relevant to the times in which programmes were written.

Historically, comedy was often used to undermine the powers that be and make important points about things happening in society at the time. Humour is a safer way of putting a strong viewpoint across and less likely to lead to punishment. Thus, *M*A*S*H* made strong political points about the futility of war and situation comedies can still make important political points, commenting on society. *The New Statesman*, *Yes Minister* and *Drop the Dead Donkey* are all British examples of situation comedies that made political comments and criticised Government policy under cover of the thirty minute sitcom format.

6. American Sitcom

There are interesting and valid points of comparison to be made between American and British situation comedies. Both countries have produced some good quality sitcoms over the years. Some groundbreaking, some controversial and some just plain funny; but differences in the production of situation comedies as well as cultural expectations also have an effect on the types of programme created.

Most American situation comedy is written by a team of writers and each series can run for in excess of 20 episodes. The concept for the programme may have come from one writer but generally a group of writers is responsible for creating a series. In Britain writers often work with comedy stars in the same way as film directors work with the same actors, so writers and actors are sometimes well known for their work together. The writing style of American sitcoms may seem a little industrial for British tastes, but the plus side of writing in teams is that American sitcoms have a much shorter production time than British programmes. In Britain sitcoms can take months to produce just 6–8 shows, but in the States an episode can be turned around in a week, so allowing writers to really get to grips with topical issues and current events. Also writing as part of a larger team is a good way for new writers to hone their talents.

Hence, British and American sitcoms have developed quite different styles. American audiences look to their sitcoms to comment on current affairs and opinion which is possibly why British audiences can sometimes find them rather moralistic. And this also means more excessive British exports like *Absolutely Fabulous* have to be watered down so as not to cause offence – the characters may be taken more seriously than intended. However, just because British sitcoms are not as immediate as American programmes does not mean they cannot make political comments; while some American sitcoms challenge audience perceptions, certainly the expectations of audiences on opposite sides of the Atlantic are different when it comes to home made comedy.

Your students may not be aware that British and American culture is very different, but it is. Britain's obsession with social class permeates a lot of situation comedy, as does the idea of the 'American dream' in the States. American situation comedies often seem to have a moral message, even those, like Roseanne and *The Simpsons*, which conservatives have criticised for their portrayals of family life.

Another interesting comparison is the broader range of situation comedies that openly discuss and portray life from different cultural viewpoints in the US. In Britain there have only been one or two situation comedies focusing on black families or issues of race, the best known of these being *Desmond's*. There is certainly not the same discussion of being Jewish in British comedy, for example, as there is in America, but then there is more focus on comedy actors from Asian backgrounds in the UK (but even this is limited). This could reflect that America has a more racially diverse culture than the UK, but it may reflect other aspects of their growth as a nation.

Comedies such as *The Fresh Prince of Bel-Air* (1990–96) and *The Cosby Show* (1984–92) were interesting because they presented highly successful upper-middle class black families. You would assume that programmes that were almost exclusively made up of black characters would discuss elements of black culture, or racism, but this only happened on rare occasions. In fact, *The Fresh Prince of Bel-Air* was much more about social class than about race.

Will Smith plays the nephew of a highly successful lawyer who becomes a judge in a later series. Will is from Philadelphia and has a much more working class upbringing; in fact, he is sent to this exclusive neighbourhood to prevent him getting into trouble. His cousins are impeccably dressed, especially the two older ones who Will generally mocks while they look down on him. Carlton dresses like an English Etonian and his air-head sister is obsessed with designer labels. At their exclusive school there are many students from different ethnic backgrounds who all get along together fine; certainly there are no problems with racism. The issue of race was rarely dealt with in *The Fresh Prince of Bel-Air* though there were the occasional episodes or sudden reference that brought the issue to the fore.

The Cosby Show was very similar but aimed at a family audience rather than the teenage audience of *The Fresh Prince*. As well as both tracing the ups and downs of rich, black families they also were largely built around the star persona of the central characters. As is common in many situation comedies Will Smith and Bill Cosby were both well known before starring in their respective sitcoms. Unusually though, Will Smith was a successful rap star rather than comedian or actor and it was *The Fresh Prince* that was the springboard for his acting career. The show began with a rap to tell the story of how the 'Fresh Prince' ended up in Bel-Air and for this target audience Will Smith's star persona as a musician would translate easily into this cool and witty character.

In some ways these sitcoms were refreshing as they moved away from stereotyping or alienating audiences from other ethnic backgrounds by always focusing on issues of race. However, there was definitely an air of idealism, rather than realism. These characters were so successful, they rarely had to deal with racism in their careers and their children attended exceedingly grand, private schools. *The Cosby Show* did attract criticism as it was seen by some to be so concerned with showing such a positive representation of a successful black family that it ignored actual racial problems and inequalities that were apparent in American culture at the time.

Families like the Huxtables and the Banks represent the relatively minor group that is wealthy, Black America. Yet here were two successful sitcoms that depicted this as if such families were common. Such examples can bring up some interesting discussions regarding ideology and institutions. Situation comedies that show families like these are perpetuating the ideal of the American dream and possibly persuading white, middle class audiences that they shouldn't worry about inequalities – just laugh along with these two situation comedies and be reassured.

Case Study: *Friends*

The principal cast of
Friends

Friends is a good focus text for students for two simple reasons: all your students will have seen it and lots will love it, and it is continuously repeated, so if need be you can set 'watching *Friends*' as homework. In addition, you can discuss elements of characterisation, representation, *mise-en-scène* and camera work; and issues of culture and idealism.

Friends no doubt became popular in part because of the lifestyle it portrayed. It reflected a new thirty-something culture where staying single is fine and having good friends is essential. For British audiences – and perhaps middle America too – the New York setting was the icing on the cake and we all dreamed of living next door to our friends, in great apartments in such a cool place. Occasional inserts of shots of Greenwich Village, the cool, hip neighbourhood of New York City, reinforced the setting, as did the trips to the coffee shop. As well as boosting the Starbucks franchise (the barely disguised model for 'Central Perk') in the UK, *Friends* offered audiences a modern ideal for young, singletons. The *mise-en-scène* in *Friends* added to the light-heartedness of the way plots and storylines are dealt with.

Surprisingly, then, *Friends* does actually deal with some quite big issues at times, such as surrogacy, infertility and family problems. But these problems don't seem to affect the characters' moods particularly badly in their day-to-day lives. No one suffers from depression; these are about the only Americans ever represented in contemporary film and TV who don't have therapists. Phoebe's character is supposed to have had a dreadful childhood but, bizarrely, her experience of homelessness and a mother who committed suicide are issues that are often referred to humourously. The only affect on Phoebe seems to be an appealing quirkiness, as whereas it would probably have driven most viewers to psychosis.

The costuming of some of the characters is also significant in *Friends*. Rachel is the sexy, rather dim one in the early episodes, always seen in short skirts and tight tops. Phoebe wore 'wacky' earrings and brightly coloured patterns to reflect her 'kooky' attitude and lifestyle; she also had 'alternative' jobs – masseuse and musician (the joke being she is a terrible musician). Costuming changed to a certain extent in the later series, but the characters retained an identifiable style, relating to their differing personalities.

Technical elements are an interesting thing to observe in *Friends*. In ensemble comedies, it is interesting to observe how the camera focuses on the whole group as much as possible, so there are many wide and long shots used, particularly in Monica's flat and the coffee shop where we are more likely to see the whole group together at once. There are also lots of shots of two characters at the same time, even if they are not an essential part of the conversation. You could discuss with your students the possible, different reasons for this. One reason, I would suggest, is to support the general socialisation that *Friends* provides. It works a lot like a soap opera, but without being depressing. In *Friends* we are continually reminded 'I'll be there for you' – in the theme music, in the storylines, with the group hugs and with the camera often focusing on more than one person at a time. As I mentioned earlier, *Friends* in some ways reflected a new generation of single thirty-somethings, but this life is not always full of friendship and fun, so this programme could provide you with some on-screen friends instead. More cynically, it might also keep the actors happy, making sure that there wasn't too much focus on one or two of the characters to the detriment of the others.

Friends became one of the most popular situation comedies of the 90s, on both sides of the Atlantic. It wasn't particularly challenging or innovative, but did reflect a changing trend in modern society and so makes an interesting case study for students. It has also, occasionally, been criticised for its lack of representation of ethnic groups, but this had little effect on its ratings.

Further Delelopments

Though many television critics and some writers are predicting the end of the situation comedy, some interesting new programmes have come out of America in recent years. I have already talked about *Scrubs*, which has a contemporary style and appeals to young audiences. *Will & Grace*, which is also discussed elsewhere, represents homosexuality in a more modern way to anything that's preceded it, mainly looking at the close relationships that women can often have with gay men.

My Name is Earl is another popular, recent show to come from America, premiering in September 2005. Jason Lee stars as Earl, a petty criminal who was run over just as he had won $100,000 on the lottery which meant he loses the ticket. While lying in hospital he decides it is karma that led to his downfall so he decides to make amends for all the bad things he has done in his life, making a list of what these are while he recovers. When his ticket turns up he is reassured that he is doing the right thing, and sees this as a sign. Each subsequent episode sees Earl finding the people on his list and follows the difficulties Earl has helping them.

The humour develops from the difficulty Earl has trying to be a good person: his old friends often try to encourage him to return to his criminal ways; people don't believe he will help them or don't want to forgive him; and it is always more complicated for him to help people than he thinks it is going to be. Moral dilemmas are the main premise of *My Name is Earl*, but the peculiar array of characters and highly polished filming techniques ensure *My Name is Earl* stands out.

Seinfeld is another highly commended recent comedy to come from the US. The show was piloted in America in 1990 and three years in, it was one of the most popular shows in America. Similarly to the style of Hancock, writer and star Jerry Seinfeld chose to make the show about characters and the minor things in life that cause major annoyance. He also added interesting supporting characters, who often played more of a part in the show than he did. The other element was the addition of Seinfeld doing a stand up routine at the beginning and sometimes the end of many of the shows. Though this sort of blurring between stand up and sitcom has been done before in *Home Improvements*, it is more subtle in *Seinfeld*. His routine would cover the issues that were to be discussed in the show but it wasn't clear if it was 'Jerry Seinfeld' the character, performing as part of the show (i.e. diegetic) or Jerry Seinfeld in his other role as stand up comedian.

Probably the most noteworthy sitcom sub-genre the US have popularised is the adult animated sitcom. The animated sitcom has been the forte of American producers, with early shows like *The Flintstones* (1960–66) and *The Jetsons* (1962–63) designed for family audiences. Since Matt Groening created *The Simpsons*, *South Park* (1997–), *Family Guy* (1999–) and *American Dad!* (2005–) have all proved popular with audiences, even though they often criticise the American institutions (the Fox Network is a regular target on *The Simpsons*).

The Simpsons first hit TV screens as an animated sitcom in 1989, though Groening initially created some shorts previous to this using the Simpson family aired during *The Tracy Ullman Show* (1987–90). Although instantly popular, it still received vocal criticism from those outraged by this 'desecration' of the American family the Simpsons represented. Unlike many family-based American sitcoms, Groening steers well away from overt moralising. His characters are flawed; even Lisa, the morally upright and academically gifted member of the family, is still prone to cheating and lying occasionally. Bart is always in trouble and Homer, the head of the household, is weak-willed, often drunk and rather stupid. Marge, the stay at home mother, is also prone to moments of weakness so no one character stands out as 'good' – just as in real life.

The Simpsons is an intelligent sitcom, parodying films and film genre, making clear reference to American culture and politics, all within an animated family sitcom. Its huge appeal has led to many celebrities guest starring as themselves, adding further to its kudos. There are often messages relating to family values in *The Simpsons* and though they have arguments and fights, moments of tenderness are often shown between the different family members. The appeal of *The Simpsons* is its ability to surprise with new plots and funny narratives, while at the same time maintaining a high standard in its characterisation and witty dialogue. After a decade the popularity of *The Simpsons* remains huge, culminating in the release of *The Simpsons Movie* on the big screen in July 2007.

South Park, created by Trey Parker and Matt Stone, was first broadcast in the US in 1997. The animation was extremely crude, intentionally so, as this was part of its cult appeal with teen audiences. Other attractions were, in no particular order, small children swearing, a singing turd and an array of racist, repressed religious fanatics and generally stupid characters. Narratives were bizarre and generally ended with the death of Kenny, always reborn again for the next episode. A film spin-off of *South Park* was also released in 1999.

The timing of these two sitcoms could have played an important role in their success. A revival in animation was evident in the 80s and toilet humour was making its mark on Hollywood comedy films when *South Park* was released, for example the success of the Farrelly Brothers' *There's Something About Mary* (1998). Whatever the reasons for their success, it seems animated sitcom is the new alternative comedy.

There have also been a series of successful comedy dramas exported to the UK over recent years, including *Sex and the City*, *Six Feet Under* and *Desperate Housewives*. Though not part of the sitcom genre per se, arguably the lines are blurring between these two forms and comedy dramas are definitely worth a mention when discussing sitcom. Making comparisons between the two has to be relevant in the classroom when looking at the development of the situation comedy genre. One of the reasons critics give for the perceived demise of the sitcom is they feel other genres like the sketch show and, especially, the comedy drama are replacing situation comedy. Though the differences between sketch shows and sitcoms are obvious, the difference with drama is more debatable, especially with the development of different styles in recent situation comedies, such as the reality TV convention of *The Office*. Some consider that comedy dramas deal with more serious themes or more complex characters. Formally they also usually last for an hour instead of half an hour. But if these are the only differences between the two genres, separating the two would rely on both sticking to tight, generic conventions which is increasingly difficult. Watching how the forms develop and observing new commissions will make interesting viewing from now on.

7. Representation

Representation is a key concept in any Media Studies course and an interesting area of study within the situation comedy form. Characters in sitcoms are rarely complex and are indeed more likely to be two dimensional or stereotypical. The aim of the sitcom is to make us laugh and although characters can be interesting and may have hidden depths, audiences are not expected to have to work hard to get to know a character.

Stereotyping refers to the simplistic portrayal of social groups within the media. Men, women, young, old, black, white: we all belong to different social groups, and within these groups have varying beliefs and understanding of our culture and place within it. Stereotypes are built up over time, around assumptions people make or comments that have been reinforced through repetition. They are ingrained within different cultures and though they can be a quick way for audiences to recognise a character type, stereotypes are arguably perjorative, and can be dangerous as they restrict social mobility through implicitly asserting a person's place in the social order.

If sitcoms are presenting us with representations of different groups in society in simplistic, stereotypical forms, there is a danger that these stereotypes will be supported within our ideology. Sitcoms in the past have been criticised for this and this could be a reason for the lack of representation of diverse groups in sitcoms today. Writers may prefer to avoid themes around ethnicity or sexuality precisely for fear of presenting characters that cannot properly represent diversity. This chapter focuses on issues around representation in sitcoms and analyses how various groups have been presented in situation comedies of the past and present.

Disability

British comedy, since Shakespeare's times, has derived humour from people with disabilities; from speech impediments to hearing problems. It seems acceptable to laugh at characters with learning difficulties or disabilities if done in a certain way. In *Open All Hours*, we were invited to laugh at Arkwright's stutter, as Granville, his nephew and assistant mocked him and some of the humour of the script was built up around this: it was clearly signalled for audiences that this was part of the comedy. In *Shameless*, a character with Tourette's syndrome causes some humour and, in *Robin's Nest* (1977–81), a sitcom set in a bistro, a one-armed Irishman employed to wash-up managed to offend two social groups in one character.

It is important that different groups are represented on television; but when it comes to comedy, there is a fine line between laughing *with* and laughing *at*, and certain audiences will find some representations offensive while others will think they are justified. *I'm With Stupid* (2005–) is the first situation comedy starring a group of disabled actors and co-written by a disabled writer. It is the result of collaboration between Daniel Peak, who wrote *Two Pints of Lager (And a Packet of Crisps)* and *My Hero*, and Peter Keeley, a young disabled writer, who originated the idea based on some of his own experiences as a disabled man.

As a quite a light-hearted situation comedy it doesn't delve into a lot of the very real issues facing disabled people in our society. But it is a breakthrough in that is rare to see the representation of disabled people in everyday situations in any kind of television programme, let alone a sitcom. The plot centres on the friendship between Paul, a young disabled man living in a residential home, and Sheldon, a homeless man, who Paul invites to come and live with him when they meet one night in a police station.

The jokes are light-hearted enough for a mainstream audience and points are made gently about people's attitudes towards disability. But with a disabled writer and cast, this programme is showing how sitcoms can positively represent social diversity in comedy, by involving those groups in the creation of those programmes rather than laughing at them without any experience of being part of that group.

Another interesting representation of disability is in Peter Kaye's *Phoenix Nights*. Brian Potter, the luckless owner of The Phoenix Club in Bolton, is wheelchair bound. Brian's disability is, in some ways, the cause of a lot of the humour in Phoenix Nights, but not in the stereotypical, simplistic ways previous sitcoms have represented disabled characters. Brian is mean-spirited, sarcastic and tight-fisted and he exploits his disability to get what he wants. However, he is also the clever, quick-witted one in the club and although things always go wrong for him, it is not because of his infirmity that we laugh, it is that he has the same trait as many central characters in situation comedy – he is not a very nice person! Brian is the most intelligent character in this sitcom, which subverts the usual representation of disabled characters. In Brian Potter we see a disabled character who doesn't 'represent' disabled people. He is not established as the voice of a group or a disabled person we laugh at. He is just a nasty, but witty, man, who happens to be in a wheelchair; and though some of the humour may involve his disability, it is not his disability that we laugh at.

This therefore brings up another difficulty within representation – how to present a character from a minority group without them becoming a symbol for that group. And although this problem may be partly one of audience reception, it is also down to the quality of comedy writing.

Social class

Social class is still a large part of situation comedy and comedy drama, as British culture has always been interested in class and regional differences. A range of sitcoms represent working class men who seek to climb the social ladder and it is their class that holds them back; for example, Del Boy and Harold Steptoe. Though we laugh at these characters, audiences are directed towards feeling some sympathy for them. Both men were born into poor families and had to struggle to keep their family together. They know their backgrounds and lack of education mean they cannot escape their environment, so they pretend to be educated and middle class, and these pretensions are part of the comedy. We laugh at them for trying to be something they are not, but we are also presented with snobbery, class systems and unfairness which some would suggest are still evident in modern British culture.

Keeping Up Appearances (1990–95) is similar, with a female central character desperately trying to climb the social ladder. Hyacinth's social snobbery and desperation to befriend the 'right kind' of people is offset against her uncouth family, who she is constantly trying to hide from. The humour, then, is not just centred on her outrageous, bullying behaviour or her silly snobbery but also the contrast between this and her quite obviously more humble background. Audience pleasure is mainly gained from the comedy of Hyacinth's behaviour but for some it could also be the thought that she could ever be a 'real lady' considering her social background.

In the US, one of the situation comedies that stands out as representing the opposite to the usual middle class 'American dream' family was *Roseanne*. This sitcom starred the stand up comedienne Roseanne Barr and ran for nine years, but was not without controversy. A lot of this centred on off-screen problems relating to who received credit for the show but some of it related to the realistic storylines often depicted.

Roseanne and her family were not the typical family represented in American sitcoms. They struggled financially and argued about money and the children. They were sexually active but not conventionally attractive and they showed what 'real life' was like for millions of Americans. Within the comedy itself, however, it was the discussion of subjects such as under age sex, drugs and a general realist approach to comedy that made it stand out. This kind of representation is rare in American sitcom; *Roseanne* stood out as a sitcom dealing with real issues that real families had to deal with in the 80s.

Some contemporary sitcoms in the UK, like *The Royle Family* and *Shameless*, also reject representations of middle class families living in huge houses, and instead offer working class – if not a new 'underclass' – representations. In some ways the programmes celebrate working class life, family values and community. Within this, though, there is crudity, reference to crime and broken families, and representations of lazy, drunken and stupid individuals. *Shameless* in particular has proved popular with teenage audiences, but again, this text can be read in different ways. Teenagers I have spoken to seem mainly to enjoy the controversial sexual scenes and references to drugs and alcohol, rather than the pertinent comments on modern culture, class and family life.

This limited number of alternatives aside, there seems to be little effort with situation comedies in the US and UK to challenge social class and dominant ideology where wealth is the most important measure of success.

Situation comedy and gender

In contemporary programming there is a greater variety of representations of women due to changes in gender roles in society. Women are not satisfied with being represented just as wives and mothers because these are not the only roles they have in society. If programme-makers are to target female audiences then they can no longer afford to present women in such stereotypical ways. Bimbos and battle axes may have been OK in the 60s in programmes like *On the Buses*, but they would not be accepted by female audiences today. As the role of women has changed, though, so has the role of men and discussions of gender should not just focus on the role of women.

Sitcoms are meant to offer settings and situations that audiences can identify with easily, so the representation of gender in situation comedy has to have some connection with how audiences view themselves. In some ways situation comedies have been challenging gender roles for a long time because a major premise in sitcoms is the challenge of power relationships. When a male character such as Basil Fawlty or Victor Meldrew is behaving like an idiot, it is their wives that we look to, to provide a balanced perspective. Often in sitcoms it is the imbalance of the status quo, the differentiating from the norm, that creates the humour.

Women may often be cooking and cleaning, but they are also often portrayed as the intelligent, in control partner – because the man is too busy having delusions of grandeur and we are laughing at him.

Sitcoms in the 60s and 70s mainly portrayed families where men worked and women stayed at home, as this reflected the norm for a great many families. In *Terry and June* (1979–87) and *Happy Days* (1974–84) from the US, we were presented with simple but caring women whose role was to look after their husbands and families, while at the same time we laughed at their naïve comments and lack of worldliness. For the sitcom the sexual revolution seemed to merely mean young attractive women could wear more revealing clothes in sitcoms like *Man About the House* (1973–76) and *On the Buses*. However, some programmes in the 70s showed couples living together who weren't married, men and women living together as friends, and even a middle class couple who worked in partnership to escape middle class expectations in *The Good Life*.

Commonly, the family is still often represented with two parents in an established marriage and, whether working or not, women are usually represented as the ones who take control of domestic chores, unless men are doing them for comic effect. Rarely do we see women successfully bringing up families on their own, though this certainly reflects modern life for many women, or men who are taking a more domesticated role in the family.

The more interesting representations of male and female relationships seem to be in programmes like *Coupling* (2000–04), which explore the complexities of modern relationships and the lack of understanding between the sexes. Representing young couples in sitcoms seems to be a more popular concept for contemporary writers than the family sitcom and allows more scope for less traditional representations.

Will & Grace and *Friends* in the US show the changing patterns of contemporary relationships and *Two Pints of Lager*, aimed at a young adult audience in the UK, shows this in a simpler yet significantly modern way. Sitcoms often deal with sex and relationships, and this involves clashes between the sexes. It is the one side's perceived knowledge of the other which causes hilarity as the man or woman involved usually have their preconceptions undermined. In some comedy shows like *Friends* this means both genders can enjoy the show as both genders are shown to be equally stupid/sensitive/witty/intelligent at various points in the series.

It is interesting to compare representations of men and women in situation comedies of the past and present, as there should be noticeable variations to comply with changes in social expectations. But surprisingly sometimes representations have not changed a great deal.

The family

Historically, the sitcom family has been depicted as one composed of a married, heterosexual couple and two or three children. Arguably, this itself becomes a stereotype. Sitcoms based around family life, though they may have extended families as in *8 Simple Rules* and *Hope & Faith*, still mainly deal with minor moral issues and the importance of family values. Confrontations and relationship problems may be dealt with but the message is always the importance of the family. In fact, even in comedies that represent more working class or even quite dysfunctional families the message always seems to be the importance of family loyalty; therefore supporting dominant ideology .

The Simpsons, for example, even though famously criticised by George Bush as not being the right kind of role model for American families, still represents a loving marriage and the importance of family. In Britain and America where the divorce rate is so high and split families the norm, it is interesting that this is not how the family is represented in situation comedy. Instead, sitcoms arguably serve to reinforce the dominant values of society – the importance of family and the stability of marriage – even those perceived to be more 'cutting edge'.

Case Study: Family-Based Sitcoms from Different Eras – *Butterflies* and *The Royle Family*

Both *The Royle Family* and *Butterflies* focused on fairly traditional families: a mother, father and two children. Both children were in their teens to twenties. In *Butterflies*, Ria and her husband have traditional roles. He is the breadwinner; she is the housewife, with a

lot of the humour focusing on her ineptitude in this role. Ria's husband, Ben, despairs as he believes his home life should be some sort of 1950s advertisement, with a perfect wife looking after the home he has worked hard to establish and a loving family environment. Instead, he has two hormonal sons in their early 20s and a wife who longs for something other than domesticity, which she is evidently not suited for.

The Royal Family's Barbara is also a stressed mother who works hard to keep her family happy. However, unlike many traditional family-based situation comedies, the family represented in *The Royle Family* are not a cosy, middle class suburban family but a crude, working class family who live on a Manchester council estate. Working class characters in sitcoms tend to be portrayed as frustrated, wanting to escape their situations or even considering themselves better than those around them. But this representation is resisted by *The Royle Family* and it is actually *Butterflies* that represents characters wishing for a different life. In *The Royle Family*, no one wants to escape their lives, no characters see themselves as trapped and unfortunate; they are just happy watching the television and spending time together.

Butterflies brings up some interesting points of discussion regarding value systems because on the one hand, we have a typical middle class family of the era, a representation people would feel they should aspire to; but on the other hand, the couple at the centre of the programme are pretty unhappy and so the audience are placed in an oppositional position to these value systems.

There is undoubtedly love within the family, so we have some common generic references to the importance of the family in both sitcoms. The main plot throughout *Butterflies*, running alongside the family discussions at the dinner table, is the flirtatious and borderline adulterous relationship between Ria and a wealthy businessman, Leonard. It is either Ria's values or loyalty to her family (or cowardice) that stops her from running away with him and so her stagnant marriage continues. But the audience throughout the series are never placed in a morally clear position to the narrative. Audiences were invited to laugh at Ria, though. She was a dreamer, who fantasised about freeing herself of the restrictions society placed on her as a respectable, married woman. This often involved considering running naked through the streets or making love in the rain, or some other brazen act of defiance; but inside Ria didn't have the confidence to become more spontaneous and certainly did not have the support of her husband. Leonard offered her a chance to escape, but Ria never took it.

Barbara in *The Royal Family*, seems generally happy with her life, though she evidently has a lot fewer material things than Ria. Never out of leggings, her hair straggly and unruly, it is clear that Barbara is too busy looking after everyone else to look after herself. Often she is the butt of husband Jim's jokes without realising it and when she does get her own back she laughs at her own cleverness, as it is so rare for Barbara to be witty. The two mothers have very different roles within these two sitcoms: Ria represents the bright, middle class woman who is frustrated that her youth and freedom seem lost. Barbara's expectations are much lower than Ria's but she doesn't feel trapped or certainly doesn't say she does; and everyone is happy plodding on with little money and hardly any life outside the home, the TV and the pub in *The Royle Family*.

Though both of these sitcoms were about families, *Butterflies* centred much more on Ria, while *The Royle Family* was about the whole family. Each episode of *The Royal Family* was set in real time, with generally static cameras giving audiences an intimate view of life with the Royles. A combination of hand-held and static camera shots reveals a detailed set, showing us Jim picking his nose or Anthony staring at the television, placing audiences at the centre of a narrative where nothing really happens, though at the end of each series there would be an important family event. On some occasions a close-up of the television would allow the audience to watch the same programme as the family. There was no studio audience or canned laughter; *The Royle Family* instead reflects the TV fashion of its times by portraying 'real life' through documentary filming

The Royle Family

techniques. It seems unlikely that this style would have worked in the time Carla Lane was writing *Butterflies*, though she was always keen to represent real issues and characters.

Butterflies combined location shooting with studio filming. It seems significant that the location scenes showed Ria's small escapades, away from the confines of her domestic life, which were filmed in the studio. Ria was almost always with her family or ineptly performing domestic duties when indoors and generally she met Leonard in a park as he represented her desire for freedom. The realism in *Butterflies* came from the feelings expressed by Ria rather than the detailed set or real time elements of *The Royal Family*. These two programmes, though both representing families with traditional family values, were different in terms of style and issues they wanted to represent. *Butterflies* was much more of a social comment on the place of women in the family where as *The Royle Family* was a celebration of working class family life.

Sexuality

The representation of gay central characters in mainstream comedy programmes has had more impact on US audiences than British ones. This is probably due to British audiences being much more used to 'camp' characters on TV, such as Dick Emery and John Humphries in the 70s and Julian Clarey and Graham Norton more recently. However, sexuality as an 'issue' is rare in situation comedy and has only recently been dealt with in the US, in programmes such as *Ellen* (1994–98) and *Will & Grace*.

Ellen was the first successful situation comedy to have a lesbian as its main character. The programme did not start out as a sitcom with a gay character as the focus, but the comedian Ellen DeGeneres, who played the central character, is gay and, 'came out' very publicly between seasons three and four in 1997. American channels are not big risk-takers because of the importance of advertising to their revenue so NBC made a brave decision to support DeGeneres in outing herself in a show. Obviously, this was seen as must-see TV and marks an important step in the portrayal of sexuality in mainstream programming. Before then only minor gay characters and stereotypes were seen in comedy shows. Cynics suggested it was a way of gaining attention when ratings were modest and whether this is the case or not it worked. The episode in which Ellen reveals she is gay ('The Puppy Episode') gained an audience of 45 million Americans as well as generating much media attention. Even in the late 1990s some groups were unhappy that a central character in a mainstream comedy was allowed to be gay, but for others *Ellen* marked an important step in accepting gay sexuality into mainstream programming.

Some would suggest though, that the show then became too heavily about sexuality and gay issues rather than Ellen, her friends and relationships. This is a common dilemma when a programme is the first to represent a minority group, and a difficult consequence to avoid. If issues are ignored writers could be accused of disregarding discrimination, but if issues are over-discussed then critics complain of over-indulgence.

Will & Grace seems to provide a more up to date twist on the representation of sexuality, desire and friendship. It centres on a narrative involving four friends, two of whom happen to be gay. Jack is very camp and quite stereotypical, but this is balanced by Will's lack of stereotypical qualities. *Will & Grace* is also very popular with female audiences because of the romantic feelings sometimes expressed between Will and Grace, which is where some felt *Will & Grace* weakened its impact in dealing with gay sexuality. Though Will was quite openly and unambiguously gay, there was an affection bordering on attraction portrayed between him and Grace. This seems to support the view that gayness can be 'cured', or could just be a lifestyle choice; but on the other hand it could, more positively, be suggesting sexuality is less of a black and white area than some would like to think.

Age

Family based sitcoms tend to portray the easiest stereotypes of different age groups: the awkward teenager, the grumpy grandad. Modern sitcoms tend to focus on people in their 20s and 30s in friendship or work-based sitcoms leaving older audiences with the increased feeling that society isn't interested in the wisdom and humour that can only be gained from experience. However, there have been significant and popular situation comedies entirely focused around the relationships and mischief caused by groups of friends in their 50s and beyond.

In the UK the nostalgic *Last of the Summer Wine* portrayed a group of retired men who got into all sorts of scrapes. The physical stunts that were part of the action belied the age of the characters, an almost indestructible group of older men who were too busy having fun to worry if they ought to be behaving more sedately.

In the US Susan Harris brought *The Golden Girls* to TV (1985–92). The narrative focused on three middle-aged women and one old woman, who shared a house in Miami. Harris, who also wrote *Soap*, specifically created characters who would challenge the myth that older women were not interested in sex by making it a major talking point in the show. The characters were all very different from each other, a cause of much of the humour. Witty and perceptive, the show won ten Emmy awards, including Outstanding Comedy Series twice. Both of these sitcoms reject the idea that at a certain age specific behaviour is expected and both established themselves as popular shows with audiences of all ages.

Race

In the 1970s the representation of ethnic minorities in comedy was pretty simplistic and focused around the problems of integration. Most characters were stereotypical and unchallenging. For example, in *Mind Your Language* a variety of adults from different countries, such as Greece, Germany, Italy and India are represented in a comedy set in an English language school. Unsurprisingly then, most of the humour was based on the characters' misunderstanding of the language, their exaggerated accents and their desire to be more 'English'. The only neutral character, without exaggerated aspects, was of course, the English teacher.

In the 80s, as the more left wing, alternative comedians gained prominence in stand up comedy and their style eventually filtered through into some situation comedies. Tastes were becoming more politically correct and audiences were no longer satisfied with crude stereotypes. Multiculturalism and minority audiences were important to channels, especially Channel 4 who had a Multicultural

Programmes department. *No Problem!* (1983–5) was the first all black production created by this department but even with its positive production values its characters were actually pretty stereotypical and one dimensional.

Desmond's, however, did manage to succeed where *No Problem!* had failed. *Desmond's* was set around a barber's shop in Peckham and in the family home of the owner, Desmond, so it had a domestic and workplace setting. *Desmond's* successfully reached a mainstream audience and dealt with being black in Britain without resorting to simple stereotypes. It was also successful in America and the Caribbean where it was broadcast on the Black Entertainment Channel (BET).

Recently though, there has been surprisingly little representation of ethnic groups in mainstream situation comedies in Britain and, as mentioned previously, writers seem to prefer to avoid representing ethnic groups rather than deal with the undoubted complexities of a multi-cultural society. If a situation comedy is to successfully portray a diverse range of representations, commissioners need to work closely with writers from these diverse communities. There are few writers that have the skill and sensitivity to write about people they have little experience of: *Desmond's* was successful because it involved black writers and actors; *Skins*, the new drama commissioned by E4 is popular with teenagers, in part because they were involved in writing it. There has never been a better time to experiment with production methods and employ new writers as digital channels offer relatively low-risk opportunities to develop new and challenging comedy. Situation comedy is still a form where these developments are possible and may impact on mainstream channels in the long term.

8. Textual Analysis

Technical aspects

It can be quite difficult to focus on technical aspects of situation comedy in part because it is easy to foreground the performances of the actors rather than the lighting, camera work, etc., that is supporting their work when analysing the genre. Nonetheless, it is an important aspect of any examination requirements. Firstly, I will summarise various aspects of technical language to ensure you and your students have a good basic grounding in moving image analysis and consider examples of how you could apply this analysis to situation comedy.

Mise-en-scène

Some situation comedies rely heavily on verbal wit and satire. Consequently, *mise-en-scène* and camera work may not appear to be as important in these programmes. But the detail of set and costuming in many situation comedies is often a large part of what makes a series identifiable and funny, whether the comedy is primarily verbal or visual.

Two good, yet very different, examples are *Blackadder* and *The Royle Family*. Each of the *Blackadder* series was set in a different historical period and in a different domestic space, from the interior of the Royal Palace to a First World War trench. The first series was quite expensive to produce due to the numerous settings used, but each series had a detailed set which provided additional visual pleasure for audiences.

The set in *The Royle Family* is very important as it gives a real sense of the iconography of working class culture. The amount of detail is evidently a large part of the poignant humour of this programme as the camera sometimes pans around the room, taking in all of the ornaments and photographs and, of course, the overflowing ashtray. The pleasure in these shots works on different levels. For some viewers the strange pictures made of coloured string wrapped around pins will make them laugh because they are so awful. Others will cringe because they remember owning one. I also think the details are probably important to Caroline Aherne, one of the creators of the programme (who also played Denise), and part of her personal memories.

Lighting

Lighting is used to create atmosphere in a scene and though it is unlikely to provoke humour by itself, lighting is undoubtedly important to create a sense of the setting which is in turn very important to the humour. Lighting is part of the *mise-en-scène*, but it is often significant enough to be considered as a distinct aspect. It establishes a colour scheme and therefore works alongside set and costume to create a desired 'look'.

High key and low key lighting might be used in situation comedies. High key lighting means the use of lots of fill lights along with the key lights so everything is brightly lit and there are few shadows. This helps to create bright daylight and will probably be associated with the more light-hearted comedies or those centred on a domestic setting.

Low key lighting uses fewer fills, so more shadows are created with definite pools of light interspersed. You might associate this with horror films and mysterious settings so it may seem strange then that you could associate this kind of lighting with situation comedies. The reason for using low key lighting is mainly because there are many comedies with a darker edge or programmes that are set in unpleasant places where low key lighting adds greatly to the set. *Father Ted*'s house, for example, has a green, dark aura inside, created by the horrible set details and the use of low key lighting.

Camera

Combined with the other technical elements of language we've discussed so far, the use of the camera can significantly affect our reading of moving images through the choice of shots and the camera's movement. The angle the director chooses to show us the action from, the depth of focus on a character's reaction and the viewpoint we are given through the choice of shot, all reinforce how the director wants us to view this particular character or situation. As highly skilled readers of moving images we are aware of conventional shots used for certain situations and dramatic effect, such as close-ups to emphasise the reaction of a character, or low angle shots to exaggerate the height of someone or something.

The way the camera moves helps to emphasise tension, excitement or brings our attention to something quickly. Panning and tilting (moving from one side to another or up and down) shows us the setting, or can emphasise size. Cameras may be mounted on cranes or tracks to film scenes from various interesting angles. A crane shot can rapidly place us in or pull us out from the action using a variety of angles, while tracking shots follow the action. Camera movement won't be as sophisticated in situation comedy as in films, but it is still used purposefully so is something you should look out for.

A common convention is to use a hand held camera, so the audience may feel they are actually 'there' following the action, or it can create a documentary effect. *The Office* mainly uses a combination of hand held cameras and static close-ups as it is a parody of a documentary, so directly copies documentary techniques. *The Royle Family* also has a fly-on-the-wall style, and uses the camera to immerse the audience in the family's life. The importance of camera work in situation comedy will depend somewhat on the importance of visual humour in the particular text. Comic suspense and slapstick humour will use close-ups and cuts between shots to build up the tension and ensure maximum enjoyment of the moment the visual humour breaks.

Because comedy sometimes breaks the rules for comic effect, the camera can be used in some interesting ways that would not be done in other television genres. For example, characters are allowed to talk directly to the camera in some situation comedies. It can also be used in other forms to break the realism and create maximum, humorous impact. For example, in one episode of *Men Behaving Badly*, where Deborah and Dorothy have gone on a sailing weekend, Gary and Tony are chatting up some girls that are visiting next door. They surprisingly accept the boys' invitation to a barbeque and then the audience see the boys doing their 'getting ready' ritual, played out with the diegetic and non-diegetic use of a Bee Gees classic.

The first shot is of the boys combing their hair in front of the mirror. The camera is static and acts as the mirror so we see the boys dancing by the mirror in time with each other, moving in and out of shot in time to the music. To end this scene, the music becomes non-diegetic again and they pelvic thrust their way towards the static camera again; then out of shot and the music fades out. It is a well choreographed piece, parodying John Travolta's *Saturday Night Fever* (1977) routine well, as Gary and Tony couldn't be less cool.

Sound

There are two main methods of separating sound in moving image analysis: sound that is internal, part of the world of the characters; and sound that is external to this world, for example, narrative voiceovers or music added for effect. The first of these is known as diegetic sound and the latter as non-diegetic sound. Situation comedies can confuse us as they can break the rules, with characters providing their own narration through their thoughts and sometimes even by talking directly to the camera, though still in character. And, as is evident from the example cited above, sound can be non-diegetic and diegetic at the same time!

Music in sitcom, as in film and drama, can be used to create appropriate atmosphere. It is often used between scenes in situation comedy, not really as sound bridges, because it wasn't present in the previous scene, but to essentially do the same job of connecting the scenes together, or seperating the comedic moments. Music can be used to create tension and often parodies horror films at dramatic moments. This seems to be particularly significant in a lot of scenes in *Red Dwarf*, where characters – or impending doom – would be announced by a deep, typically dramatic flourish of music. *Blackadder* also announces villainy with music similar to that which accompanies silent movies.

Sound effects can also be important in situation comedy, particularly with forms like slapstick. The thwack of a pan hitting Eddie's face in *Bottom* or the exaggerated punch sound underlines the cartoon style violence prevalent in such situation comedies and helps ensure the violence is understood in its comedy context.

Another thing to consider when analysing situation comedy is whether the sound is parallel or contrapuntal. Parallel sound is when music is used that suits the mood of the action but contrapuntal is the opposite of this. Contrapuntal sound can be used in drama or horror to add an even more sinister edge, such as when children's nursery rhymes are sung in frightening scenarios, but it can also be used in comedy to create further irony and comedy effect.

Theme tunes to situation comedies often become well known signifiers of the style of the comedy. The excellent, punk style version of 'The Young Ones', for example, totally reinvents the twee sound of Cliff Richard, who is of course greatly admired by Rik, one of the main characters in the show. The melancholic Oasis track 'Half the World Away', which is heard over the opening credits for *The Royle Family*, clearly evokes the programme's – and the band's – Manchester roots.

Another significant element of sound to consider when discussing situation comedy is the inclusion, or exclusion, of canned laughter. A tradition of sitcoms since the earliest days, some consider canned laughter to be false and intrusive. Certainly it is a uniquely interesting aspect of the genre. We generally accept it as part of viewing a sitcom but can we imagine canned screams working in horror films? It could be suggested that the inclusion of canned laughter is part of the socialisation of sitcoms. It is always nicer to share a joke with others. It also encourages audiences to understand the humour; the canned laughter acting like a prompt card for audiences.

Editing

Film and TV programme-makers approach editing in the same way because editing plays an important part in setting the pace of any narrative. They decide how to connect shots and the order in which to place shots after filming and again, this plays a vital part in the construction of the narrative; deciding what will happen and where.

Shots can be placed together consecutively so that one event logically follows from the next but there will be gaps in the telling of a story as there are some details an audience can assume has happened without actually seeing it happen. For example, if we see a character walking down the stairs and then the next shot is of the same character on a bus, we can fill in the gaps of them leaving the house and walking to the bus stop ourselves. These gaps are referred to as the 'ellipses' between shots.

There are a number of different styles of editing that can be used to join the shots together after the footage of a programme has been gathered. These are the following:

1 The **straight cut** is the clean cut between shots that as an experienced audience we don't really notice.

2 The **fade out** is where the shot slowly disappears into blackness (though occasionally white may be used). The fade is generally used to show us that one section of the narrative is being left behind while we refocus on another section. It can signify the closure of a particular narrative thread and also the passing of time.

3 The **dissolve** is where one shot fades into another. It can also be used to show the passing of time, but because two shots are connecting, a dissolve edit can signify the connection between one part of the narrative and another, unlike the fade.

4 A **wipe cut** is where a black or white screen comes on from the side, pushing the previous shot off the other side or it may also come from the top or bottom of the screen. This is sometimes used in situation comedy as it has a humorous edge to it. It might signify the conflict

between two sides of a family, for example.

5 A **jump cut** is unlikely to be used in situation comedy, unless it is parodying an action film or horror film as that is the genre which tends to use this style of edit. It is basically where the shot appears to jump forward to get closer to something. It has a jolting effect both on the screen and the audience, as it draws our attention to something quickly and makes us slightly jumpy.

Particular types of edit are conventionally used to create certain effects. They may appear more frequently in some genres than others, as stated. This may be worth mentioning when observing how editing is used in the situation comedies you choose to study, as you may find this is significant in the meaning the writers are intending to create.

Wildly contrasting styles of editing are unlikely to be used in most situation comedy as they tend to stay within a 'realistic' environment. Wipe cuts might be used to break these rules and dissolves are commonly used to show the passing of time or a change in setting, but generally when looking at editing you mainly notice how it affects pace.

Straight cuts will be used most often, so look for how often a shot changes. It will be used more often with a big cast, or to build excitement/drama, or to see characters' reactions to events or each other. Generally, the more edits that are used, the faster the pace of the narrative, so particularly tense or exciting atmospheres will be created.

Narrative

Discussion of the narrative consists of two different aspects: the story and, more specifically, the structure of that story. The narrative structure refers to a construction of events in a particular order with links that tie together events separated by time and space. Audiences are quite sophisticated in their ability to work out clues and piece together elements of a plot, as part of the pleasure of a narrative is working out the answers to the questions you first posed before the narrative gets to that point.

Within a situation comedy we are often given narrative cues to help us enjoy the build up to the climactic situation or joke. Sitcoms often use omniscient narratives, where we the audience know more than the characters, so we can anticipate the humorous disaster about to unfold. When a restricted narrative is used this provides a different viewing experience for an audience, a different exposition of the humour.

A narrative shapes material in terms of time and space – it defines where things take place and how quickly. Commonly the pace will pick up in the latter stages of the narrative, as it reaches its climax. Most narratives are structured on the Todorovian principle of equilibrium–disruption–new equilibrium, but situation comedies don't always have to follow normal rules, depending on their style.

Another important element of the narrative in situation comedy is comic suspense, which is often connected to the positioning of the audience in relation to the narrative. The audience anticipates the humour that is about to unfold, usually because they know more than the characters in the sitcom. A good illustration of this is in the 'Yuppy Love' episode of *Only Fools and Horses*. The audience sees that a bar flap has been lifted to allow the barman to collect glasses, but Del Boy is looking in the opposite direction. When Del then leans back, commenting on how cool he and Trig should behave, he falls straight to the floor. This is hilarious for lots of reasons – the performance of the actors, the dialogue, but also the comic suspense created by the audience knowing what the characters do not.

Below are two examples of textual analyses to support similar work you may carry out with your students.

Red Dwarf, Series 1, Episode 1

Red Dwarf

As the very first episode this programme stands out in the series as very different from the rest. It had to establish how Dave ends up stranded in space, the last ever human being alive. So although the programme begins with a big cast, it ends with the small ensemble that would be the basis of the first two series. The sequence discussed is from where Dave has to go into cryogenic stasis to his realisation of what has happened.

The *mise-en-scène* is simple to begin with. Grey walls, tables and uniforms along with low key lighting means nothing stands out. This could signify the 'normality' of this scene. *Red Dwarf* is a working vessel with a mix of crew you might find in any factory. Dave is the mischievous skiver and Lister is the social climber. When Dave has to go into stasis, though, downlighting is used to create the mysterious interior of the chamber. The addition of a colour and Dave's bright shirt places additional emphasis on the chamber.

Lighting and colour continue to be used to good effect in this sequence. When Dave is released he walks around the whole ship and although the main areas are still cast in a dull grey hue, walking through another section red and blue lights signify an engine room, typical of the sci-fi genre's use of colour, which cast bright shadows on the main character. Interestingly, when Dave arrives at the drive room the monitors are the same colours as Dave's Hawaiian shirt.

Camera work is used appropriately to create moments of tension: a close-up of the Captain's face when Dave has to choose between giving up his cat or going into stasis for 18 months; a zoom in and out from the close-up of Dave's face as he waves from the stasis chamber. Also, a typical shot of the exterior of the ship, commonly used in the *Star Trek* (1966–69) series, indicates to the audience that time has passed before we return to the shot of Dave in the chamber.

Music is used throughout the sequence to set the mood and to aid continuity. The same piece of music begins when Dave is placed in the chamber, continues throughout the exterior shot of the ship and as Dave is released from the chamber, so the audience's attention is maintained. They know something else significant is happening while Dave is frozen in time, as the tense music plays throughout. The music then changes as Holly, the ship's computer, informs him that the rest of the crew are dead, to the accompaniment of a single electric guitar, increasing the dramatic impact of the news.

Throughout this scene there are a number of jokes, some built up gradually and others throwaway quips. The main joke is Dave's slow realisation that the whole crew is dead. Holly has to repeat himself over and over again as Dave adds yet another crew member to the list of who might be dead. Eventually Dave stands still, the music stops and he says, 'Wait. Are you trying to tell me that everybody is dead?'

Blackadder, Series 3, Episode 4 ('Sense & Senility')

Blackadder the Third

After the expensive first *Blackadder* subsequent series were filmed in studios, not simply because of the expense but also because star Rowan Atkinson believed the location filming was having a negative effect on the comedy. A change of writer for the latter three series evidently influenced the characterisation and dialogue, with Ben Elton replacing Atkinson as Richard Curtis's writing partner. *Blackadder the Third* uses the traditional three camera set-up, limited sets and a laughter track, as it was filmed before a studio audience.

In this episode the Prince Regent employs two actors to help him write a speech to re-gain public support when he is attacked by an anarchist. He rejects Blackadder's offer and mocks him in front of the arrogant actors so Blackadder decides to leave. Of course, he returns when he is proved right; the Prince cannot cope with only Blackadder's simple aide Baldrick to take care of him. This extract referred to, is where Blackadder leaves and Baldrick overhears the actors rehearsing and thinks they are plotting against the Prince.

The sequence starts in the kitchen where Baldrick is preparing some food and Blackadder is saying his goodbye. Straight away the focus on wit and sarcasm are evident. Blackadder starts with what sounds like a fond farwell, only to follow it with 'but we both know it would be an utter lie, so I will confine myself to simply say, sod off'.

Atkinson's timing and Blackadder's sardonic nature are key to any sequence, but the comedy is heightened here as Baldrick, for once, criticises his master when he thinks he has left, calling him a 'lazy, big nosed, rubber-faced bastard'. This is not only funny because it is so rare but because audiences familiar with Rowan Atkinson, the performer, are aware his 'rubber face' is part of his comic performance in other comedy projects, like *Mr. Bean* and *Not the Nine O'Clock News*.

Further humour in the use of language is Baldrick's mix up with the lines he heard from the actors and Baldrick's ironic repetition of the Prince's criticism of him: 'Who me? Mr thicky Black thicky adder, thicky.' The clever use of language and wit is arguably the most important aspect of the show, but for Blackadder's clever lines to work so well, they have to be in the context of the stupidity of the other characters; and in each series, Blackadder has always had these characters to bounce the jokes off.

The *mise-en-scène* in this sequence is detailed, with candles in each setting, reinforcing its period setting but also adding to the shadowy subject matter in this scene. Most of the *Blackadder* series used quite low key lighting to convey the various historical settings represented. The first series was set in the Middle Ages and *Blackadder Goes Forth* in the First World War, so the darker colours and lighting suit the mood of the times. The second and third series are much more opulent reflecting the tastes of the royals Blackadder serves (Queen Elizabeth I and the Prince of Wales, respectively). But it is significant that his living quarters are much darker in terms of lighting and colour, probably to reflect the black heart of the central character.

The music is used in this sequence to add comic, dramatic tension. When Baldrick overhears the actors 'plotting', a deep brass instrument underlines the melodrama of the scene. Then later, as he is hiding under the table with the Prince, further dramatic music alongside the exaggerated echoing footstep sounds, signifies their impending doom. Of course, when the door opens with an anti-climactic squeak Blackadder is revealed and his timing is impeccable – not to save the characters, as they think, but with the response to his earlier suggestion that they could not last five minutes without him. He looks at his pocket watch and declares: 'Good evening your highness. Five minutes and twenty-two seconds precisely. Baldrick, you owe me a groat'. The equilibrium is restored, as Blackadder once again reasserts his place in the group.

Conclusion

In this *Guide* I have discussed programmes I have personally enjoyed (which I think is a valid starting point for anyone) as well as looking at comedies from the past and present. As with all Media Studies topics, it is important to look at texts, in this case situation comedies, in the context in which they were made and viewed. Different audiences will appreciate situation comedies for different reasons and it will be difficult to avoid discussing tastes, target audience and social and historical context with your students when approaching this subject.

Hopefully, you won't avoid these debates. Studying situation comedy will allow your students to look at texts they enjoy and maybe even appreciate texts they may not have yet experienced. In the end though, engaging them in discussion and debate is the best way to secure their learning; whether they enjoy watching Hancock or not, after studying various texts and their styles, they might be able to say why.

Within your debates, you should also consider the place of the sitcom in contemporary scheduling. Armando Iannucci, creator of *The Day Today*, delivering a lecture in his role as Visiting Professor of Broadcast Media commented: 'Just as comedy shows get more daring and varied in format and technique, and just as audiences get more and more sophisticated in the breadth of comedy they're willing to watch, viewing figures are in decline. Less comedy is being made for the mass audience channels of BBC1 and ITV, while the commissioning of comedy shows is increasingly in the hands of TV professionals from outside comedy production under pressure from advertisers and schedulers not to take risks' (*The Guardian*, Stephen Armstrong, Monday, 30 January 2006 www.technologyguardian.co.uk (accessed 23 July 2007)).

New writing talent does seem to be striking out to produce more abstract and challenging programmes for audiences, in drama and comedy; but if channels are happy to stick with reality shows and quiz shows because these are popular and cheap to produce, and sitcoms are not, there is little scope for the revival of the mainstream sitcom. The sitcom form may not be dead but if channels and networks aiming at young audiences are not keen to commission or broadcast them, it could well be a format in decline.

For anyone over the age of 30, situation comedy probably played a large part in their years of family viewing or even listening. If younger generations are not experiencing the form now, they will not be reminiscing about classics from their past in years to come. The form is not the problem – tastes change and styles develop to suit new, ever demanding audiences. If the sitcom is to survive it has to be relevant and flexible enough for a range of audiences and platforms.

Bibliography

Dunbar, B. (2002) *Comedy Films: A Teacher's Guide*, Leighton Buzzard: Auteur.

Essen, M., Phillips, M. and Riley, A. (Consultant, Ashton, J.) (2004) *GCSE Media Studies for WJEC*, Oxford: Heinemann.

Jancovich, M. and Lyons, J. (eds) (2003) *Quality Popular Television*, London: BFI Publishing.

Lewisohn, M. (2003) *The BBC.co.uk Guide to Comedy*, London: BBC Books.

Malik, S. (2002) *Representing Black Britain: Black and Asian Images on Television*, London: Sage Publications.

Martin, R. (2000) *TV for A-Level Media Studies*, Oxford: Hodder & Stoughton.

Mills, B. (2005) *Television Sitcom*, London: BFI Publishing.

Neale, S. and Krutnik, F. (1990) *Popular Film and Television Comedy*, London: Routledge.

Wagg, S. (ed.) (1998) Because I Tell a Joke or Two: *Comedy, Politics and Social Difference*, London: Routledge.

Websites

The British Sitcom Guide www.sitcom.co.uk
Various pages accessed 2007

The Museum of Broadcast Communications www.museum.tv
Anderson, C. 'I Love Lucy'
http://www.museum.tv/archives/etv/I/htmlI/ilovelucy/ilovelucy.htm
Date accessed 30 July 2007

Kassel, M.B. 'Father Knows Best'
www.museum.tv/archives/etv/F/htmlF/fatherknows/fatherknows.htm
Date accessed 30 July 2007

Screenonline www.screenonline.org.uk
Fiddy, D. 'Clement and La Frenais'
http://www.screenonline.org.uk/people/id/462833/index.html
Oliver, J. 'Croft and Perry'
http://www.screenonline.org.uk/people/id/479645/index.html

Lacey, N. and Stafford, R. (2002) Comedy Films for GCSE Media, Notes
for Teachers and Students
http://www.itpmag.demon.co.uk/Downloads/GCSEComedy.pdf
Date accessed 20/06/06

Lewisohn, M. (2003) The BBC.co.uk Guide To Comedy
www.bbc.co.uk/comedy/guide

Old Time Radio Show Catalogue www.OTRCat.com
Date accessed: 10 July 2007

Radio Days www.whirligig-tv.co.uk/radio/index.htm
Date accessed: 10 July 2007

Taflinger, R.F. (1996) Sitcom: What It Is, How It Works
www.wsu.edu:8080/~taflinge/sitcom.html
Date accessed: 27 June 2007

Widner, James F. (1998) Comedy Central, Radio Days
www.otr.com/comedy.html
Wikipedia http://en.wikipedia.org/wiki/Sitcom
Date accessed: 16 June 2007

The Young Ones
www.nostalgiacentral.com/tv/comedy/youngones.htm
Dateaccessed: 8 January 2006